DRAMA CLASSICS

The Drama Classics series aims to offer the world's greatest plays in affordable paperback editions for students, actors and theatregoers. The hallmarks of the series are accessible introductions, uncluttered texts and an overall theatrical perspective.

Given that readers may be encountering a particular play for the first time, the introduction seeks to fill in the theatrical/historical background and to outline the chief themes rather than concentrate on interpretational and textual analysis. Similarly the play-texts themselves are free of footnotes and other interpolations: instead there is an end-glossary of 'difficult' words and phrases.

The texts of the English-language plays in the series have been prepared taking full account of all existing scholarship. The foreign-language plays have been newly translated into a modern English that is both actable and accurate: many of the translators regularly have their work staged professionally.

Edited until his early death by Kenneth McLeish, the Drama Classics series continues with his aim of providing a first-class library of dramatic literature representing the best of world theatre.

Associate editors:
Professor Trevor R. Griffiths
Professor in Humanities, University of Exeter
Dr Colin Counsell
Senior Lecturer in Theatre Studies and Performing Arts

DRAMA CLASSICS *the first hundred*

*The publishers welcome
suggestions for further titles*

DRAMA CLASSICS
TARTUFFE

by
Molière

translated and introduced by
Martin Sorrell

NICK HERN BOOKS
London
www.nickhernbooks.co.uk

A Drama Classic

This translation of *Tartuffe* first published in Great Britain as a paperback original in 2002 by Nick Hern Books Ltd, The Glasshouse, 49a Goldhawk Road, London W12 8QP

Reprinted 2005, 2011, 2012

Copyright in the introduction © 2002 Nick Hern Books Ltd

Copyright in this translation © 2002 Martin Sorrell

Martin Sorrell has asserted his right to be identified as the translator of this work

Typeset by Country Setting, Kingsdown, Kent CT14 8ES
Printed in the UK by Mimeo Ltd, Huntingdon, Cambridgeshire PE29 6XX

A CIP catalogue record for this book is available from the British Library

ISBN 978 1 85459 637 6

Introduction

Molière (1622-1673)

Jean-Baptiste Poquelin (later known as Molière) was
baptised in the St-Eustache church, Paris, on 15 January
1622, but the precise date of his birth is not known. Both
his parents were in the upholstery business, enjoying
considerable success and wealth. Between 1633-1639
Molière was educated at the Jesuit Collège de Clermont,
now the Lycée Louis-le-Grand. In 1642, he was a law
student in Orléans, and in the following year he
renounced his succession to his father as *tapissier du Roi*
(upholsterer-royal), preferring instead to join the newly-
formed Illustre Théâtre company in Paris. In 1644, he
adopted the name Molière, and this marks the beginning
of his illustrious career as actor-manager-playwright. His
first full-length play, *The Scatterbrain*, was put on in 1655.

The company at first toured the provinces, then returned
to Paris in 1658 and shared the Petit-Bourbon theatre with
the Italian commedia dell'arte players. Molière also
received the patronage of the King's brother, Philippe
d'Orléans. 1659 saw the great success of *The Pretentious
Ladies*. In 1661, the company was forced to move to a
different theatre, the Palais-Royal. In 1662, Molière
married Armande Béjart, then aged around 20. She was
either the daughter or the sister of Madeleine Béjart, with

whom Molière had set up the Illustre Théâtre some twenty years before. Molière's acutely pertinent and highly successful *The School for Wives* was given its premiere in 1662. The next year, he was granted a royal pension of 1,000 livres, and in February 1664 the King himself acted as godfather to his first child, Louis. In May of the same year, the first version of *Tartuffe* was given privately before the King, but was immediately banned for public performance.

In 1665, Molière's company became the Troupe du Roi, and his annual royal pension was raised to 6,000 livres. In the early part of 1666, Molière became seriously ill with pneumonia and had to give up acting for many months. The summer of that year saw *The Misanthrope* and *Doctor in Spite of Himself*. Then, in 1667, *Tartuffe*, renamed *The Impostor*, was given a public performance. 1668 saw first productions of *Amphytrion, George Dandin, The Miser*, 1669 *Monsieur de Pourceaugnac*, 1670 *The Would-be Gentleman*, 1671 *Scapin's Tricks*, 1672 *The Bluestockings*. Molière's last play, *The Hypochondriac*, opened on 10 February 1673, but, by its fourth performance, on 17 February, Molière's illness, probably tuberculosis, had become critical. He was performing the title role of Argan, the hypochondriac, and by all accounts doing so with great energy and gusto. Then, near the end of the performance, in the third interlude, he was taken violently and suddenly ill, but he managed to struggle through to the end of the performance. He was rushed back to his house in the rue de Richelieu, where he died shortly after. He was buried on the 21st, in the St-Joseph cemetery, during the night – the penalty for not having made, in the presence of a priest, a death-bed denunciation of his actor's life.

Tartuffe: **What Happens in the Play**

Orgon, a rich *bourgeois* living in Paris, has taken into the family home a certain Monsieur Tartuffe, a down-and-out he had encountered at church, and who manifested all the signs of deep religious piety. Act 1 opens with a raging quarrel between various members of the household, one of whom – Madame Pernelle, Orgon's mother – is for Tartuffe, the remainder against him, as they consider him an impostor. Through the servant Dorine, we learn that Orgon, who had served the King with valour and distinction in the recent civil strife (known as La Fronde), has become obsessed, under the influence of Tartuffe, with religion and the virtues of the pious life. When Orgon makes his first appearance, having been away a couple of days, his only concern is to find out how Tartuffe has been. Orgon learns that Tartuffe is in excellent health, eats and drinks heartily, and sleeps heavily. On the other hand, Orgon's wife Elmire has been quite ill, but that detail is of no concern to Orgon. Cléante, Orgon's brother-in-law then tries to reason with him in a scene which lays out the deep divide of the times between religion and *libertinage* (free thinking, open-mindedness, often interpreted by its opponents as irreligion and atheism). Cléante is wasting his breath, however. Orgon is locked into his vision of Tartuffe as saintliness personified. He cannot see how ridiculous he appears, nor the frustration and distress he is causing within his family.

Act 2 opens with an interview between Orgon and Mariane, his daughter of marriageable age. He plans for her to wed Tartuffe. Not only is this prospect intrinsically awful, but Mariane is in love with a young man called

Valère. Dorine then has a go at Orgon, not mincing her words, but this produces only rage and stubbornness in her master. Dorine then assures the over-submissive Mariane that she will act on her behalf to thwart Orgon's designs. Valère arrives, and instead of agreeing a plan of action, the two lovers launch into a pointless argument, resolved only by Dorine's exasperated intervention. After that, there is agreement that everything must be done to ensure that Mariane and Valère do indeed marry each other.

Act 3. Elmire has asked for a meeting with Tartuffe, in order to plead the cause of the young lovers. It seems that she is the only person in the family to exert any influence over Tartuffe. Orgon's impetuous young son Damis insists, against wiser counsels, that he should listen in secret to the meeting. Tartuffe makes his first entrance. On seeing Dorine, he slips into the character of the religious ascetic, and requests that she cover her provocative cleavage. After Dorine's choice words of reply, Tartuffe and Elmire begin their conversation. But it takes an awkward turn, for Tartuffe quickly steers it to his own obsession, the physical charms of Elmire, and how to find a discreet way of satisfying his desire for her. At this delicate moment, Damis bursts in, having heard everything, and declares that he will unmask the treacherous impostor. Orgon then arrives, Damis blurts out the whole story, and Tartuffe, challenged by an incredulous Orgon, plays a brilliant psychological card by beating his breast and agreeing wholeheartedly with Damis's accusations, even adding that he, Tartuffe, is more evil than anyone knows. This skilfully contrived statement of the naked truth produces the desired effect – Orgon turns not on Tartuffe but on his son, cursing him before sending him packing. Then he comforts Tartuffe, who deftly returns to the subject of Elmire. Orgon's prompt response is that, far from avoiding her, Tartuffe henceforth must spend as much time as possible in her company. His final, mad decision is to disinherit his son, and make his whole estate over to Tartuffe.

By the opening of Act 4, Orgon has become totally despotic. Cléante confronts Tartuffe in an attempt to persuade him that he would do better to refuse the inheritance and not marry Mariane. In vain. Tartuffe fobs Cléante off with vague replies, then abruptly leaves. Mariane pleads with her father not to make her marry Tartuffe. She would rather die in a convent, but Orgon stiffens his resolve. So Elmire decides that the only way of opening Orgon's eyes is to engineer an encounter between herself and Tartuffe, and lead him on in the hope that his true nature will be disclosed to Orgon, hiding under the table. Tartuffe arrives, and he and Elmire begin a negotiation in which she pretends to offer to start an affair with him. Tartuffe, at first mistrustful, slowly relaxes, and asks for immediate proof of Elmire's good faith. To her objections to adultery on religious grounds, Tartuffe has replies of sickening casuistry. She then threatens to unmask him to her husband, to which Tartuffe responds contemptuously that Orgon can be hoodwinked with the utmost ease. Elmire seems to give in to Tartuffe, and asks him to go out and check that the coast is clear. Orgon emerges from beneath the table, his eyes at last opened. Tartuffe re-enters, and Orgon orders him to leave his house forthwith. Tartuffe points out, however, that, since *he* is now the owner, the papers having been signed, it is for Orgon and his family to go. But the true position is even worse, for Orgon hints at a further complication, to do with a certain strong-box which should be in his possession.

Act 5 opens with the revelation that the strong-box contains papers belonging to Orgon's friend Argas, whose sympathies for the Fronde has made him an enemy of the State, and caused him to flee. But, so that he could legitimately say, if questioned, that he did not have the box, Orgon has entrusted it to Tartuffe. This is Tartuffe's ultimate weapon against Orgon, evidence of treachery. The position for the family is potentially catastrophic. Damis returns, and is reconciled with his father. Madame Pernelle arrives, still convinced that Tartuffe is being wrongly accused. A bailiff, Monsieur Loyal, enters with orders to evict Orgon, his family and their possessions by the morning. He has with him a gang of heavies to make sure that this indeed happens. Madame Pernelle at last sees the truth. Valère runs in to warn Orgon that he is in the gravest danger, as Tartuffe has gone to denounce him to the King. Valère has organised transport, money and a safe house, but too late. Tartuffe arrives with a law officer, ostensibly to arrest Orgon. Tartuffe now is playing the role of loyal subject of the Crown, whose only duty is towards the King. But Louis XIV, the all-seeing Sun King, all along has been watching Tartuffe, who in fact is a notorious confidence trickster. The King has simply been waiting for Tartuffe to make a false move. Thanks to his loyal service during the Fronde, Orgon is pardoned for shielding Argas, and his estate restored to him by royal decree. The law officer leads Tartuffe off to prison. Orgon has had a lucky escape, and learned his lesson. The play ends with his promise that his daughter will be married to Valère, the emblem of sincerity.

Versions of the Play

The first performance of *Tartuffe*, in a version, now vanished, composed of the first three acts, was given at Versailles before the King (Louis XIV) on 12 May 1664. However, as it was already generally known that the play's subject had to do with religion and hypocrisy, representations were immediately made to the King by the Archbishop of Paris and the First President of the Parliament to have it banned. Yielding to their pressure, and perhaps in order not to offend his mother, Anne of Austria, who by this time had become devoutly religious, and who also was seriously ill, the King informed Molière that he would not authorise any public performances of the play. Private productions, however, were sanctioned, and a few took place. The play was also read aloud in the presence of an influential church dignitary, who saw in it no matter for offence.

By 1667, Molière judged that circumstances had changed sufficiently to allow him to try again, and, following a conversation with the King, the tone of which did not seem discouraging, Molère put on an altered version of the play. It opened on 5 August 1667, with a new title, *The Impostor*. The eponymous hypocrite, now clearly portrayed as a man of the world, and with no connection to the Church, was renamed Panulphe. However, Molière had misjudged. Once again, his play was banned, once

again on the grounds that the theatre must not be allowed
to deal with matters of religion, whatever the author's
intentions, whatever the play's intrinsic merits. Molière
appealed to the King, but was fobbed off with hollow, if
sympathetic, words. Ironically, the play was now banned
totally. Even private performances were proscribed.
Seemingly, the explanation was that, for reasons of
diplomatic and political necessity, the King was concerned
not to antagonise the Church hierarchy any further.

But, by January 1669, the influence of the religious groups
hostile to Molière had waned so rapidly that the ban on
Tartuffe became impossible to sustain. Molière now had no
effective enemies, and the play, in its present five-act form,
opened without protest on 5 February, its original title
restored. It ran for several weeks, to much acclaim.

Molière's own Preface to the play, and the three *Placets*
(petitions, in effect) he wrote to the King between 1664 and
1669, give a good sense of the controversy and of Molière's
deep frustration.

Tartuffe has been in the French repertory ever since 1669,
and is one of Molière's most celebrated and frequently
performed plays.

Religious Background to the Play

The absolute monarchy of Louis XIV (who reigned from
1643 to 1715) was indissolubly tied to the Church. A King
might be enthroned by divine right, but he had to work with
the Catholic Church, especially when, as in mid-17th
century France, it was so much in the ascendant. If not, a

King risked punishment in this world and the next. The two
powers effectively running France, one temporal, one
spiritual, needed one other, whatever mutual mistrust might
exist. After the Council of Trent (1545-63), when France
had refused to accept the Inquisition, Rome set up secret
societies to perform the Inquisition's function, namely, the
promotion and protection of Catholic orthodoxy and
Church interests. By the time of Molière, the secret societies
were becoming increasingly worried by *libertinage* – not so
much sexual promiscuity as open-minded intellectual
curiosity. *Libertins* did not accept religious dogma as
unchallengeable truth. Some *libertins* adopted a quiet sort of
agnostic and pragmatic humanism, as opposed to ordained
faith, creed and superstition. Others, more daringly,
proclaimed themselves free not only of imposed systems of
thought, but constraints of personal and social behaviour
too. Their self-conscious amorality famously was taken by
Don Juan to extremes of lucid and cynical defiance of
convention. The consequences of his activities, in which
godlessness and blasphemy were more crucial in his doom
than seduction and licentiousness, form the subject of
another of Molière's great plays, the darkly disturbing *Don
Juan*, of 1665. However, in *Tartuffe*, and through the
mouthpiece of the rational Cléante, Molière pleads the case
for the well-behaved end of the *libertin* spectrum. In vain:
Establishment France had resolutely tarred all forms of
libertinage with the same atheistic, anti-social brush. The
penalties for proven *libertinage* could be dire indeed, ranging
from imprisonment to torture and death.

The arch-enemy of the *libertins* and of *Tartuffe* was the
Compagnie du Saint-Sacrement (Company of the Blessed

Sacrament). This body had been set up in 1627 to do charitable work, which indeed it accomplished. But it turned into a police force of theology, operating in the shadows, with spies and strong-arm men, like a modern State Intelligence service. Under the cover of its charitable work, the Company identified 'enemies', and denounced them to Church and lay authorities alike. Its power was frightening, and Molière would have had every reason to fear it. Only two years before the first *Tartuffe*, a Parisian lawyer had been burned at the stake for writing verses deemed not to have shown sufficient respect for the established Church – and this was far from an exceptional case. Nor could Molière rely any more on the King's protection, as Louis did not want to displease his ailing mother, the ultra-devout, disapproving Anne of Austria.

However, there was considerable hostility to the Company of the Blessed Sacrament among important sections of French society, certain prominent politicians included. So, while the Company's powers were formidable enough to hound Molière through his early career, and to have *Tartuffe* banned in 1664 and again in 1667, by 1669 the position had been reversed. Officially banned in France, and no longer backed by Rome, the Company's teeth were drawn. Molière was free to resurrect *Tartuffe*. From that time on, its success was assured.

The Early Hostility to the Play

Why was *Tartuffe* banned? Molière's Preface and the three *Placets* to the King give a good sense of the issues. Molière claims that his intention never was to mock men of good faith, genuine God-fearing believers. Nor was his target the Church. His attack was on impostors and confidence-tricksters. It should be remembered that the times were propitious for Tartuffe and his like. France was recovering from the civil war of 1648-53, known as the Fronde, in which Louis had had to assert his authority over the parliamentarians. The fall-out was a McCarthyesque climate of suspicion and recrimination. Threats to secular and religious authority were seen everywhere. Orgon, fundamentally a sincere and devout Catholic, and who had served the Crown well during the Fronde, fell for the fashionable idea that a family of standing should have its own *directeur de conscience* (its own moral and spiritual mentor). On occasions, this mentor would even come to live in the house, as does Tartuffe. The situation Molière depicts was not exceptional, and if it seems quaint in our secular age, perhaps the current fad for therapies of various stamps, and gurus, personal trainers, personal shoppers etc. fulfils a comparable function, modern pedlars of older spirituality . . .

Orgon is half-mad not because he has a mentor, but because he has chosen a fraud. In his Preface, Molière insists that he has taken the greatest care from the very start to establish that Tartuffe *is*, incontrovertibly, a phoney. This is crucial; by the time Tartuffe makes his entrance, at the beginning of Act 3, we understand his character without any possible ambiguity. Indeed, everyone within the play does too, except Orgon and his mother. Moreover, Molière says, since the aim of comedy should be to correct human vices by exposing them to laughter, his play is beneficial as well as inoffensive. So how could genuine religion and religious groups object?

The response was that the theatre had no business dealing with religion; Molière was guilty of criminal trespass. Leave theology to God's appointed, that was the implication, whatever the political subtext. Certainly, no French comedy before had taken on religion in quite this way, but the fact that drama had many of its origins in the Church – physically, in churches – was conveniently disregarded. The real reason for upholding the ban on *Tartuffe*, of course, was that Molière had scored a bull's-eye. Hypocrisy flourished in the Company's heyday. (Charpy de Sainte-Croix and the Abbé Roquette, to name but two, were well-known religious impostors). So Molière had to be silenced. Even when, in the 1667 version, he toned things down by changing Tartuffe's name to Panulphe and painstakingly built up a picture of an irreligious and fraudulent man-about-town, down to his attire (little bowler hat, long hair, and wearing a sword), it made no difference, nor did the fact that Louis's devout mother had died in 1666. It was only in January 1669, once the so-called Peace of Rome had been concluded, that the climate was right for *Tartuffe*, and it was sanctioned for general performance.

Original Staging

The first performance of *Tartuffe* was given as part of a seven-day royal festival in the gardens of Louis XIV's palace at Versailles. This festival, a multi-faceted spectacular called *Delights of the Enchanted Island* (*Plaisirs de L'Ile enchantée*), took place in the presence of the King and six hundred of his courtiers. Molière was commanded to provide the theatrical entertainment, which included some of his comedy-ballets, and, on the festival's penultimate day, *Tartuffe*. The setting for the festival was a sizeable area of parkland. A contemporary engraving indicates that Molière's plays would have been performed on a ground-level semi-circular apron, directly in front of the King, and behind which was an ornamental pond complete with artificial sea-creatures. The style of acting would have been fairly static, but gestural too. The role of Tartuffe, whose mask of hypocrisy has become his natural face, surely must have required the actor to play without too much movement, and close to the audience.

Of the Paris productions of *Tartuffe* in the late 1660s, we know something about both decor and costume. In view of 17th-century French drama's insistence on the unities of time, place and action, the set needed to remain unchanged all through. An account by Molière's stage-designer describes a simple room with two armchairs, a table and a table-cloth, two torches and a slapstick (the last, probably used by the law officer, in the final scene, as a token of authority). The character of Orgon, played by Molière himself, wore the costume of a rich bourgeois – doublet and hose, garters, black cape lined with watered silk and embroidered with English lace, and slippers adorned in a similar fashion.

A Comedy of Character and Illusions

The sense given so far of *Tartuffe* is of a controversial, dark play about hypocrisy and deception among unedifying people. What is comic about that? The plot itself, as so often in Molière, is a convenient peg, and not intrinsically comic: will the daughter marry the young man of her dreams against a domineering parent's wish? The answer is yes, and had it not been – which seems more than likely until the very end – the play *ipso facto* would have left the realms of comedy to become something more troublesome. Indeed, grim disaster for Orgon and his entire family is averted only by the last-minute intervention of the King, in a *deus ex machina* which has displeased most commentators, on the grounds of its assumed implausibility (an assumption which has been challenged, and which will be considered later). Clearly, an element of *Tartuffe*'s comedy derives ultimately from the Italian *commedia* which Molière knew well. The set plots and stock characters of farce are not far away – they never are in Molière, from the earliest farce, *The Flying Doctor*, to the final comedy of character, *The Hypochondriac*. Thus, there are trace elements of Pantaloon in both Orgon and Tartuffe, of the Inamorato in Valère, the Inamorata in Mariane, and of Harlequin, Scapino and the Soubrette in Dorine. Then, also deriving from so-called 'low' comedy, there are the *lazzi*, set-piece situations developed according to the demands of each individual play (comparable, say, to a riff in jazz). The most glaring instance is Orgon crouched under the table, but there are other moments too, usually involving Dorine.

Yet Molière absorbs such coarse features into a mix which produces an altogether more refined comedy, like that of the later *Misanthrope*. Now we have comedy of character, of smiles rather than belly laughs, smiles at the absurd disproportion of two characters, each distorted by obsession and self-deception. While such characteristics could easily lead to serious and permanent consequences, in *Tartuffe* they do not. Order and proportion are restored, if only just in time. Crisis is averted because Orgon finally comes back to earth, whereupon Tartuffe is unmasked. Such damage as has been done is reparable. Lessons will have to be learned by everyone – even Tartuffe himself, for whose eventual rehabilitation Cléante expresses rather pious hopes in his closing speech. Everything once again has assumed correct proportions; temporary aberrations have been rectified. Those on stage as well as in the auditorium can smile with relief. Clearly, we are in the realm of comedy. It has to do with a 'natural' order – people *being* who they really are. Take Orgon: here is a respected citizen, loyal servant of the Crown, well-loved family man, genuinely devout, but who, for reasons which Molière only allows us to guess at – the loss of his first wife, perhaps, the excursions and alarums of the Fronde? – has *temporarily* lost all judgement in his obsession with a confidence trickster. The old cliché is pertinent – *he is not himself*. His cantankerous obstinacy has now become dangerous. His name itself surely is intended to be informative. Seemingly derived from Greek *orgè*, meaning 'anger', coupled with the Spanish augmentative *ón*, 'Orgon' signals a strongly choleric temperament. And indeed, we see the man deal with his family generally in angry mode. He even says, at one point, that his greatest pleasure is to provoke people to anger. As is true of other characters in Molière's theatre (Alceste in *The Misanthrope* is a powerful example), Orgon's condition is presented in terms of the so-called humours, in which 17th-century medicine still substantially believed. However, change is possible, and he can be cured, his imbalances corrected. If (to adapt Henri Bergson's terms) he can allow his *living*, natural self to see off his *mechanical*, blindly obsessional other self, then both he and his family can smile and laugh again, and so will we, the audience. In the end, of course, this is precisely what happens, thanks to Dorine and some of Orgon's family. Orgon emerges from his brainstorm a saner, wiser man. Unlike another famous madman, Don Quixote, the re-establishment of proportion and lucidity heralds a viable future, in harmony once more with a worthy past self, which had been temporarily obliterated.

The same goes for that vivid, if minor character, Madame Pernelle, Orgon's mother, whose own tightly-shut eyes are the last to be opened. And then, those characters who suffer from no delusions, who are not intrinsically comic, but who are at risk of permanent damage in the world according to Tartuffe, are also saved from catastrophe. Elmire, the good wife spurned by her husband in favour of a charlatan, only just avoids committing the metaphorical suicide of sleeping with Tartuffe, something Orgon has been unconsciously encouraging, Freudians take note. Damis, the wild, banished son, is brought back in from the cold and reconciled with his father; Mariane, the insipid daughter, neither has to marry Tartuffe nor disappear for ever into a convent, but instead gets Valère, the man of sincerity, the deliberate antithesis of Tartuffe; Cléante, the slightly priggish mouthpiece of a considered and well-behaved *libertinage*, is vindicated; and the splendid Dorine, non-family but scarcely below stairs, and impelled by love and unerring common sense, restores order in the scrambled minds of Orgon, Mariane and Valère.

In terms of self-deception, obsession and erratic behaviour, even Tartuffe is comic. Imagine the religious ascetic, the spiritual man, a hollow-cheeked desert-dweller and eater of stones, perhaps, or a gaunt silhouette wrapped in the raven's wing of a cassock. For two whole acts, Molière keeps Tartuffe off-stage to make us (and the Catholic Church of 1660s France) quite aware that we are dealing with nothing better than a hypocrite who will not even look the part. The celebrated *And Tartuffe?/ Poor man!* scene (Act 1, sc. 4), prepares us for a well-fed, ruddy-faced individual. Molière allows no ambiguity; there is nothing remotely devout about Tartuffe, the fleshy enthusiast of the flesh. His very name is a signal; 'tartuffe' derives from the Italian for 'truffle', but also, by extension, it connotes a bulbous nose. Plus which, the use of 'tartuffe' to mean 'two-faced swindler' is attested well before Molière's time. The comic associations of the name were therefore apparent to his contemporaries. And yet, the voluptuary with the funny name and, possibly, funny nose wants to impress all as a self-flagellating, hair-shirted hater of the world, who later will denounce Orgon's family for enjoying innocuous social gatherings. The mis-match between fact and fiction is so well-prepared that, when finally Tartuffe makes his first entrance, we instantly see the comedy of the sybaritic body in the ascetic's garb. However, doubly important, it is not just Orgon and Madame Pernelle who have got Tartuffe wrong, it is also Tartuffe *himself*. The play is built as much on the theme of *self*-deception as of the deception of others. That is obvious in the case of Orgon. But when Tartuffe, the urgent sensualist, tries to seduce Elmire, the casuistry he comes out with persuades one person only – Tartuffe.

Here, as perhaps at some other moments, he may genuinely fall for his own rhetoric. But, in the field of professional hypocrisy, he is a beginner, despite his considerable history in the trade. Elmire sees through him, as do all the other characters bar one, and as does the audience. Tartuffe is clumsy and inconsistent. What grand master of hypocrisy would make a first entrance like Tartuffe's? The consummate hypocrite would not *say* that he wore a hair-shirt and thrashed himself, he would either do these things, or else make people believe that he did, by means of insinuation or silence. He would look and act the part of a man who whipped himself while saying or implying that he did *not* do so. The fact that Tartuffe succeeds – almost – is not down to his skill. He is just lucky that the person with power, Orgon, is so astonishingly blind. From Tartuffe's entrance, from his first two lines, he is scarcely credible, and after the ensuing short exchange with Dorine, any possible credibility is lost. His demand that Dorine hide from him her bosom, a temptation he must not be made to face, not only shows his insufficiency as a hypocrite, but also ironically reveals what he is trying to conceal, the carnal lust which will be the linchpin of the drama about to unfold. He opens his account, therefore, with a monumental blunder.

In Act 2 scene 2, there is a short exchange between Orgon and Dorine which encapsulates, perhaps as well as any, the play's pervasive theme of illusion. In it, Orgon gives as one reason for his admiration of Tartuffe that the latter, though now impoverished, had once been a man of substance, or, to use a term which indicated good social rank rather than good manners, a gentleman. Now, isn't it odd that this claim, if it represents the truth, should ever have come to light? Orgon can only know it because Tartuffe has fed it to him. The result: Orgon resolves to restore Tartuffe to his former 'rightful' social position. But, morally, this should not be an aim for either man, both of whom are supposed to aspire only to transcendental purity. No, what Molière neatly exposes is Orgon's failure to understand either Tartuffe or himself. Orgon is not only obsessive, he is muddled and self-contradictory. And what is revealed about Tartuffe is not much different. In view of the *dénouement*, and the law officer's speech, it is almost incredible that Tartuffe really had ever been a gentleman of means. But his decision to leak this (dis-)information to Orgon is misjudged. The consummate religious hypocrite would not bring *sinful* ambitions to the attention of those he is trying to deceive. The risk in Tartuffe's case – slight, admittedly – is that Orgon will move from indignation to suspicion. For, even if Orgon fails to put two and two together, Tartuffe should know that he is likely to blurt it out to his family. Tartuffe thinks that Orgon is so stupid he will always be duped. However, the master hypocrite would know that his unmasking could happen in an unguarded moment of over-confidence – Tartuffe's hubristic experience, exactly.

The controlling feature of Tartuffe's psychology might be described as a misunderstood conflict between passion and self-control. Molière gets dramatic tension from this opposition, as Tartuffe twice moves from cold calculation to rash excitability and back again. This pattern describes his attempt to seduce Elmire, followed by his successful attempt to retrieve the situation, inducing a false security which allows a second assault on Elmire, whose consequences he aims to turn to his advantage by denouncing Orgon to the King. In both set-pieces, we see that Tartuffe is enigmatic and even complex. For, either he has genuinely persuaded himself that his own sensuality is without sin – not impossible, given that some mid-17th-century casuists were able to argue this position – or, unthinkingly, he is letting lust eclipse caution. At first sight, the latter position does not seem *that* stupid. After all, Tartuffe appears to have the ultimate weapon – blackmail. He reckons that Orgon's involvement in the Argas affair has given him the trump card. But that, of course, turns out to be Tartuffe's final and costliest error, since the King has been charting his criminal activities, waiting to pounce. Admittedly, Molière's use of the King's intervention is there largely, and quite crudely, to flatter Louis. This was understandable; Molière was desperately keen to consolidate the young King's patronage. As subsequent developments showed, Molière had powerful enemies, and therefore needed the best ally of all. Yet, the manner of Tartuffe's unmasking does have dramatic validity. Although this may be a minority view, some critics argue that his downfall is the predictable result of his misjudgements, as opposed to a clumsy dénouement invented by a playwright who has run out of ideas. All through the five acts, the argument runs, Tartuffe's inconsistencies have been carefully set out, sometimes obviously, sometimes subtly. Tartuffe's erratic judgement, which lands him in trouble on those occasions he *forgets himself*, steadily paves the way for the outcome Molière provides. The play's structure, then, has internal logic, and holds good to the end.

The play's profoundly comic characters are Orgon and Tartuffe. It is their illusions about other people, about each other, and about themselves, which make them comic. We enjoy observing their illusions, the more so as finally they are destroyed, to everyone's benefit. That the play does not end on an ominous note is due to these two protagonists. But what of the others? Dorine is lively, clear-sighted and possessed of an acerbic tongue; her repartee is richly amusing. But she is not strictly a comic character, in that she is not divided against herself by self-delusion. As the cliché has it, we laugh with her, not at her. On the other hand, the hot-headed Damis lacks measure, and that provokes laughter – until, of course, the consequences of his rashness threaten to bring everything crashing down on himself and others. Madame Pernelle, Orgon's dramatic double, and the ironically-named Monsieur Loyal have entertaining cameo roles, but as characters they are not sufficiently developed to do more than amuse. In the final analysis, it is the deluded Orgon and the self-deluded Tartuffe, symbiotically joined for most of five acts, who control the comedy of the play. While neither man has a sure grasp of reality, at least they both believe in the same illusion – Tartuffe himself. Despite the potential for a serious, even tragic outcome, in Orgon's blindness and Tartuffe's single-mindedness, these two central figures remain comic. Order is restored; Orgon sees clearly once more, and the possibility is floated that Tartuffe will drop his mask once and for all, and become a good citizen.

Language

A striking aspect of Molière's language in *Tartuffe* is the
way in which a powerful, dangerous and vicious subject is
couched in the elegant conventions of Classical French.
Nowhere, perhaps, is this better demonstrated than in the
two seduction scenes between Elmire and Tartuffe. The
substance is electrifying – eroticism, adultery, betrayal –
but the expression is controlled, careful, refined as a
courtly dance. The finest moments, arguably, are those
when Tartuffe employs the chaste language of religion in
the service of his lust, something which did not help
Molière's cause during his quarrels of the 1660s.
Elsewhere in the play, especially when Dorine is on stage,
the language is less contrived, more secular, though never
earthy or vulgar.

Like many of Molière's plays, *Tartuffe* is in rhyming
couplets, with alternate feminine/masculine rhymes. A
feminine rhyme involves the mute, or unvoiced, *e*, as in
the play's first two lines, 'délivr*e*', 'suivr*e*'; a masculine
rhyme is made by voiced vowels, as in ll.3 and 4, '*loin*',
bes*oin*'). The line length is twelve syllables, the
Alexandrine, prescribed by Classical French poetics. To
the English ear, even sometimes to the French, this
measure can sound monotonous and stilted; it needs
judicious handling, by writer and actor alike. Translators
into English, as a rule, reduce their line to ten syllables,
and one can see and hear why. From Pope onwards, there
has been a dislike for the Alexandrine's serpentine length.
Even allowing for the rhetorical tradition of French, in
which elaborate expression does not have to submerge
sense, some of Molière's lines in *Tartuffe* seem excessive,

occasionally padded out. His rhymes in the main are unobtrusive, but 1,962 lines of them can be overbearing if not delivered with variation of rhythm and emphasis.

In this translation, I have used free verse, with occasional rhyme and assonance. My aim has been to produce dramatic language, relaxed but not crude, which can be spoken easily while remaining purposely a little contrived. Many lines are short, some very, but all of Molière's text is accounted for. I have aimed to strike a compromise between naturalism and stylisation. I have not given the play any new or updated context, nor changed any names; we are still in 17th-century Paris. The sense Molière gives of a snake-pit in a drawing-room requires conversational dialogue within a verse structure, but I have provided one moment of stilted language in measured and rhyming verse. This is the law officer's speech (Act 5 scene 7), which I have given in decasyllabic lines, rhyming ABAB, CDCD, etc., to acknowledge the view that the *dénouement* is contrived. A stage production could emphasise this contrivance of expression by, for example, exaggerating lighting and/or sound effects, or by having Louis XIV descend, in character, onto the stage, or by projecting his image onto a screen . . .

For Further Reading

There is a vast array of information of all kinds on Molière, his life and his work. Inevitably, much of the most important material is in French. A substantial proportion of the best recent writing in English on Molière has been in the form of scholarly articles published in specialist journals. The internet will help identify and locate them.

One of the most helpful critical editions of *Tartuffe* is the one edited by R. Ledésert and R. Wilson in the Harrap's French Classics series. First published in 1949, it has gone through several editions since. Although the text is in French, there is a full introduction and notes; besides that, Molière's own Preface and his three *Placets au Roi* (Petitions to the King) are included. The most obvious and useful guide to *Tartuffe* is H. Gaston Hall, *Molière: 'Tartuffe'* (Edward Arnold, Studies in French Literature, no. 2, 1960), a succinct and interesting monograph on the play. Among the several books in English which discuss *Tartuffe*, the following, chronologically set out, are worth consulting: W.G. Moore, *Molière, a New Criticism* (O.U.P., 1949); J. Cairncross, *New Light on Molière* (Geneva, 1956); J. Hubert, *Molière and the Comedy of the Intellect* (University of California Press, 1962); J. Palmer, *Molière* (Blom, 1970); A. Eustis, *Molière as Ironic Contemplator* (Mouton, 1973); H.C. Knutson, *Molière: an archetypal approach* (University of

Toronto Press, 1976); J. Kasparek, *Molière's 'Tartuffe' and the Traditions of Roman Satire* (University of North Carolina at Chapel Hill, 1977); W.D. Howarth and Merlin Thomas (eds), *Molière: Stage and Study* (O.U.P., 1978); Nathan Gross, *From Gesture to Idea* (Columbia University Press, 1982); H. Gaston Hall, *Comedy in Context* (University Press of Mississippi, 1984); J. Gaines, *Social Structures in Molière's Theater* (Ohio State University Press, 1984); H.C. Knutson, *The Triumph of Wit* (Ohio State University Press, 1988); P.H. Nurse, *Molière and the Comic Spirit* (Droz, 1991); V. Scott, *Molière: a Theatrical Life* (C.U.P., 2000).

The reader with a reasonable command of French should listen to an audio-cassette recording of two talks, each some twenty minutes long, one on the religious background to *Tartuffe*, the other on the theme of illusion in the play. They are written and read by the late J.D. Biard, and the cassette is published in the Exeter Tapes series by Drake Educational Associates, St Fagan's Road, Fairwater, Cardiff CP5 3AE. Both talks are expert and absorbing, and have informed certain aspects of the present introduction.

Ariane Mnouchkine and her Théâtre du Soleil in Paris have made an imaginative film about the life and death of Molière. Simply entitled *Molière*, it gives a moving, if slightly fanciful, account of the playwright's life, and of conditions in the theatre of 17th-century France. This film was issued in 1986 as a video cassette by Proserpine Editions.

To all critics listed above whose work has helped in the preparation of this introduction, I wish to record my acknowledgement and sincere thanks. In particular, I owe a debt of gratitude to my colleague at Exeter, Dr Elizabeth Woodrough, who has given me much encouragement and support over the years, as well as invaluable insights into 17th-century French drama. Her work in this field is much admired by the academic community, and her forthcoming book – a new appraisal of Molière – will be essential reading. Finally, I dedicate this book to my mother, and thank her for highlighting, among other things, the subtlety of one line in particular of Molière's original, and certainly one of the most difficult to put into English: Tartuffe to Dorine, 'Couvrez ce sein que je ne *saurais* voir'. My italics pinpoint the problem – how to render the auxiliary verb, whose usual meaning, 'to know', clearly will not do. Molière's use is almost out of the reach of English, but, I hope, not quite.

Molière: Key Dates

1622	Birth of Molière. Precise date not known. Baptised 15 January in Paris, the son of Jean Poquelin, merchant upholsterer.
1633?-9	Educated at Jesuit Collège de Clermont (now the Lycée Louis-le-Grand).
1642	After brief law studies, obtains his *licence* in Orléans.
1643	June, joins the recently-formed theatre company, the Illustre Théâtre, Paris, 1644. Adopts the name Molière.
1645-58	After serving prison sentence for debt, Molière and troupe tour provinces. Enjoy patronage of the Prince de Conti, 1653-57.
1655	Molière's first full-length play, *The Scatterbrain (L'Etourdi)*, produced in Lyons.
1658	Molière and his company return to Paris. Share Petit-Bourbon theatre with the Italian commedia dell'arte players. Enjoy patronage of the King's brother, Philippe of Orléans.
1659	18 November, successful production of *The Pretentious Ladies (Les Précieuses ridicules)*.
1661	Company moves to Palais-Royal theatre. 23 June, successful production of *The School for Husbands (L'Ecole des maris)*.

1662   20 February, Molière marries Armande Béjart, aged about 20. December, *The School for Wives (L'Ecole des femmes)*.

1663   Molière receives royal pension of 1,000 livres.

1664   May, three-act version of *Tartuffe*. This is then banned but is followed in November by the full five-act version, performed in private.

1665   February, *Don Juan* (withdrawn shortly after).

Molière's company becomes the Troupe du Roi, and annual pension increased to 6,000 livres.

14 September, *Doctor Love (L'Amour médecin)*.

1666   January-February, Molière seriously ill. 6 June, *The Misanthrope*. 6 August, *The Doctor in Spite of Himself (Le Médecin malgré lui)*.

1667   Public performance of *Tartuffe* banned; renamed *The Impostor*; further ban.

1668   13 February, *Amphytrion*. 18 July, *George Dandin*.

9 September, *The Miser (L'Avare)*.

1669   5 February, first authorised public performance of *Tartuffe*.

1670   November, *The Would-be Gentleman (Le Bourgeois gentilhomme)*.

1671   14 May, *Scapin's Tricks (Les Fourberies de Scapin)*.

1672   March, *The Bluestockings (Les Femmes savantes)*.

1673   10 Febraury, *The Hypochondriac (Le Malade imaginaire)*. 17 February, death of Molière.

TARTUFFE

MADAME PERNELLE, *mother of Orgon*
ORGON, *husband of Elmire*
ELMIRE, *his wife*
DAMIS, *his son*
MARIANE, *his daughter, in love with Valère*
VALÈRE, *in love with Mariane*
CLÉANTE, *brother-in-law of Orgon*
TARTUFFE, *religious impostor*
DORINE, *maid to Mariane*
MONSIEUR LOYAL, *a bailiff*
FLIPOTE, *maid to Madame Pernelle*
LAW OFFICER

The action takes place in Orgon's house in Paris

ACT ONE

1. MADAME PERNELLE, FLIPOTE, ELMIRE, MARIANE, DORINE, DAMIS, CLÉANTE

MME. PERNELLE. Flipote, let's go.
  I want to see the back of this mad family.

ELMIRE. Slow down, we can't keep up with you.

MME. PERNELLE. Good – I've had enough of your
  'concern'.

ELMIRE. We only want to do what's best.
  Why the tearing hurry?

MME. PERNELLE. It's a madhouse here. I'm appalled.
  No one listens to a word I say,
  There's no respect for anything at all.
  It's sheer and utter bedlam. I'm leaving.

DORINE. But if . . .

MME. PERNELLE. You like the sound of your own voice too
  much, my girl.
  Servants should keep their thoughts to themselves.

DAMIS. But . . .

MME. PERNELLE. You, my lad, are an adolescent fool,
  Take it from your old granny.
  I've warned your father a thousand times

    That you'd turn out bad,
    And be a thorn in his soft flesh.

MARIANE. I think . . .

MME. PERNELLE. His sister now,
    Who cultivates an air of mystery . . .
    Stop trying to play the innocent, my dear.
    Still waters may run deep, but with you,
    Deep just means stagnant.

ELMIRE. But mother . . .

MME. PERNELLE. You may be my son's wife, but
      I don't like
    Your way of doing things.
    Stepmothers should set a good example.
    Their poor mama, God rest her soul,
    Did a much better job.
    You squander money – just look at your clothes.
    You're got up like a princess! I'm sorry
    If this offends you, but when a woman's
    Thinking only of pleasing her husband,
    She doesn't go around dressed like that.

CLÉANTE. But after all . . .

MME. PERNELLE. I defer to you, since you're her brother.
    I even have some time for you.
    But, if I were in my son's shoes,
    I'd ban you from this house.
    You preach the virtues of a kind of life
    Which no right-thinking person could accept.
    That's how I see it; excuse my bluntness.

DAMIS. Well, your Tartuffe no doubt is glad . . .

MME. PERNELLE. He's a thoroughly good man.
  You should show him respect. I won't have
  Hotheads like you trying to do him down.

DAMIS. Am I supposed to sit back and let this fraud
  Criticise us all and do as he pleases?
  We're not allowed to make a move
  Without his gracious permission.

DORINE. The Gospel According To Tartuffe
  Says everything's a sin. No one can even smile
  Unless *he's* cleared it first with God.

MME. PERNELLE. That's how it ought to be.
  He wants to guide you all to Heaven.
  Be like my son, and you'll come to love him.

DAMIS. No. Not my father, not anything
  Could make me think well of him.
  I'm sorry, but that's how it is.
  Everything that reptile does makes me seethe.
  Personally, I can't take much more.
  We're heading for a major showdown.

DORINE. It's a scandal how this nobody's
  Taken us over. When he first arrived,
  He looked worse than a scarecrow.
  He didn't even boast a pair of shoes.
  Now, he's so puffed up he thinks he can dictate
  How everyone should behave in this house.

MME. PERNELLE. God give me patience! You'd do better
  To follow his pious example.

DORINE. In your mind, he's a saint. But can't you see
  His actions are pure hypocrisy?

MME. PERNELLE. Hold your tongue!

DORINE. Two thousand testimonials
  Wouldn't make me trust him, or his servant.

MME. PERNELLE. I'll reserve judgement on Laurent.
  But his master's truly devout.
  You only damn and blast him
  Because he sees straight into your souls.
  But it's sin he hates, not the sinner,
  And what spurs him on is his love of God.

DORINE. If that's the case, why does he lock
  Our doors against all visitors?
  Why does a simple social call
  Make him fume with rage?
  Do you know what?
  I think he's jealous of Madame Elmire.

MME. PERNELLE. That's enough. Mind what you say.
  It's not just him who disapproves . . .
  Comings-and-goings at all hours,
  Carriages lined up at the gates,
  Crowds of noisy servants,
  It's not gone down well round here.
  I'd like to give you the benefit of the doubt,
  But don't forget, tongues are wagging.

CLÉANTE. You won't stop people talking, Madame.
  It would be a sad day if we gave up our friends
  For fear of fatuous gossip.
  Even if we tried, do you think

We could silence everyone?
Malice is a fact of life.
It's best to rise above it.
Let's try to lead blameless lives
And turn a deaf ear to tittle-tattle.

DORINE. Our neighbour Daphne and her pathetic husband,
Could they be the ones bad-mouthing us?
Those who live in the most fragile glass-houses
Always cast the first stone.
The slightest whiff of some imagined *liaison*,
And they're onto it.
They spread rumours with the greatest relish,
Twisting facts to fit their theories.
They paint people as black as they can
To camouflage their own activities,
Put up smoke-screens, play the innocent,
Hoping to deflect the criticism
Coming their way – and rightly so.

MME. PERNELLE. You're deliberately missing the point.
I heard the other day that Orante –
Christian virtue personified –
Utterly condemns the company you keep.

DORINE. Oh yes, she lives austerely,
But put it down to her advancing years.
She's prim and proper, since she has no choice.
In the days men were all over her,
She pulled out all the stops.
But now her eyes have lost their sparkle,
She's dumping society before it dumps her,
And shrouding her sad reality

In a veil of so-called principle.
That's how flirts who've had their day
Try to adapt to their new condition.
There's just one outlet for their bleak despair:
Professional prudery.
So these virtuous women dish out disapproval,
And tut-tut everything in sight.
They come down hard on immorality,
Not from altruism, but out of spite.
They cannot bear to see another woman
Having fun the way they can't do any more.

MME. PERNELLE.

These fantasies keep Dorine happy, no doubt,
But I don't intend to go on
Listening to her diatribes all day.
I demand to have my say.
The best thing my son ever did
Was to bring that holy man among us.
God sent him here to rescue
This household from the brink.
Take heed of what he says. He chastises
Only when you need chastising.
These visitors, these balls, this flippancy
Are the devil's work.
You should discuss theology, but no,
It's who did what with whom, and when, and where.
You vilify your neighbours;
Slander rages like a forest fire.
Even sensible people lose their heads
When those poisonous *soirées* are in full swing.
As some professor said the other day:

It's a veritable Tower of Babylon,
The way you people babble on.
And then, to prove his point, he . . .
(*Indicating* CLÉANTE.) Why are you sniggering?
If you want to laugh, go and find your ghastly friends,
And don't . . . Goodbye. I've said what I wanted to;
The scant regard I had for you has gone.
I shan't set foot in here again
For a very long time.
(*Shaking* FLIPOTE.) Stop day-dreaming, girl.
On your feet, we're off.

2. CLÉANTE, DORINE.

CLÉANTE. I'm staying out of range, in case she wants
    To go on castigating me. That old lady . . .

DORINE. Old! . . . Pity she didn't stay to hear you
    Call her that! She'd have said: He's got a nerve,
    To describe someone so youthful that way!

CLÉANTE. She's worked up for no reason;
    It's her obsession with Tartuffe!

DORINE. That's nothing compared to her son.
    You'll see, he's a million times worse.
    In the recent disturbances, he may have been
    Reliable, brave, loyal to the Crown,
    But now he's fallen for Tartuffe,
    He's in a world of his own.
    He calls him 'dear brother', and loves him

Ten times more than his own wife and children.
Tartuffe alone knows all his secrets;
Tartuffe alone controls his actions;
Tartuffe excites him more than any mistress could.
He coddles and caresses him,
Sits him at the head of the table,
And claps with joy while Tartuffe stuffs himself.
The best portions always land up on his plate,
And when he burps, it's: 'Fetch a doctor, quick!'
(*Molière's note: it's a servant speaking.*)
He's mad about Tartuffe, Tartuffe's his god,
His whole life. He worships him, quotes him
All day long. Tartuffe works miracles,
His every word's an oracle.
He's got Monsieur Orgon dancing on a string;
He uses any mask to take him in.
His stern words pay him handsome dividends,
But still he goes on castigating us.
Even his servant, that prophet of doom,
Thinks it's his right to lecture us.
He raids our rooms, eyes rolling, mouth foaming,
And throws out all our beauty preparations.
The other day, the two-faced toad ripped up
A hankie he found inside my book of prayer.
He said I was committing the mortal sin
Of mixing the sacred and profane.

3. ELMIRE, MARIANE, DAMIS, CLÉANTE, DORINE.

ELMIRE. You were right not to come out there
    And listen to her ranting on . . .
    My husband's just got back;
    I'm going upstairs to make myself look nice.

CLÉANTE. I can't stay long; but I must say
    A quick hello before I leave.

DAMIS. Talk to him about my sister's marriage.
    I think Tartuffe's against it,
    And is doing all he can to prevent it.
    You know why I'm keen it should go ahead.
    Valère, my sister Mariane's fiancé,
    Has a sister of his own, who means everything
    To me, and if . . . But here he is.

4. ORGON, CLÉANTE, DORINE.

ORGON. Well, if it isn't my brother-in-law.

CLÉANTE. Good to see you. I was just leaving.
    How was it in the country? Still no rain?

ORGON. Dorine, tell me how . . . Cléante, I'm anxious
    To know how things have been while I was away.
    (*To* DORINE.) What's happened these last two days?
    Nothing untoward? Is everyone well?

DORINE. The minute you left, Madame ran a fever
  Till almost bedtime. Dreadful migraine too.

ORGON. And Tartuffe?

DORINE. Tartuffe? On tip-top form.
  Bursting with health.

ORGON. Poor man!

DORINE. By evening, she felt very sick,
  And couldn't bring herself to eat.
  Her migraine just got worse and worse.

ORGON. And Tartuffe?

DORINE. He crossed himself,
  Then devoured a pair of partridges,
  Followed by some mutton stew.

ORGON. Poor man!

DORINE. The whole night long,
  Madame didn't get a wink of sleep.
  Her fever flared up badly.
  We had to sit with her till morning.

ORGON. And Tartuffe?

DORINE. Feeling pleasantly drowsy,
  He hauled himself up to his room,
  Flopped into bed, went out like a light,
  And was dead to the world till breakfast-time.

ORGON. Poor man!

DORINE. We finally persuaded Madame
  To let a doctor bleed her,
  Which thankfully improved matters.

ORGON. And Tartuffe?

DORINE. With great courage and self-discipline,
    Not thinking at all of himself,
    He knocked back a litre of Bordeaux
    To make up for the blood Madame had lost.

ORGON. Poor man!

DORINE. Anyway, both are on their feet again.
    I'll pop upstairs and tell your wife
    How concerned you are for her.

5. ORGON, CLÉANTE.

CLÉANTE. She's making fun of you, Orgon,
    And, *entre nous*,
    Not without good cause.
    Have you quite taken leave of your senses?
    How can one man have such a hold on you
    That everything else goes out of the window?
    Not content with scraping him
    Out of the gutter, you now . . .

ORGON. Please, enough.
    The fact is you don't know him.

CLÉANTE. So you say,
    But to find out what sort of man . . .

ORGON. If you knew him as I do,
    You'd not have the slightest doubt.
    This is a man . . . a man who . . . a man!

He radiates serenity.
He makes one see how rotten the world is.
When I'm with him, I'm transformed.
He's taught me to kill my feelings of love
For everything and everyone.
Now, my own brother, children, mother, wife,
Could die, I wouldn't lose a moment's sleep.

CLÉANTE. How very human.

ORGON. Ah, you should have been here when I first saw him.
You'd have been bowled over, just like me.
Every day he'd come to church and kneel down
Close to me, his face pure and gentle.
The congregation would watch him,
So impassioned were his prayers and supplications.
He'd sigh and weep, stretch out his arms,
Throw himself down on the icy floor,
And when I rose to leave, anticipate me
To proffer holy water at the door.
Laurent, his acolyte, told me all about him,
How poor he was.
I'd try to give him money, but he'd blush
And hand me back a bit of it.
'No' he'd say, 'that's too much. Take back one half.
I don't deserve your charity.'
I'd refuse, so then, before my very eyes,
He'd give it to the poor and needy.
Anyway, God willed that I should take him in,
Since when things have gone from strength to strength.
He keeps an eye on my interests, specially
My wife. To safeguard my honour, any man

With the slightest twinkle in his eye, he tells me,
He's *that* protective. But he goes further;
The least desire he counts a sin;
The slightest peccadillo's a major scandal.
The other day, he denounced himself – why?
Because, at prayer, not only had he caught
A flea, but he'd killed it with too much rage.

CLÉANTE. Have you gone completely mad,
Or are you trying to make a fool of me?
This is such tosh . . .

ORGON. You wouldn't be a closet atheist?
You're beginning to sound like one.
I've warned you before,
You'll get into hot water at this rate.

CLÉANTE. You people always talk like this.
Because you're blind, the whole world should be too.
An open mind, for you, equals irreligion.
Those of us who won't worship false idols
Are heretics in your book.
But your scaremongering won't work.
I know where I stand, and so does God.
People like me aren't taken in by hypocrites
Or impressed by cardboard heroes.
Real men of courage, when they're put to the test,
Get on with things without any fuss.
The same goes for true believers, whose example
We should follow – they don't go round banging their
    drum.
True belief and phoney faith are not the same thing;
Why can't you spot the difference,

See the real face behind the mask?
Sincerity and sham; truth and appearance,
There's no distinction for you.
You confuse the shadow and the substance,
Counterfeit money and true coin . . .
Human beings! What a strange lot we are,
Never straightforward or natural!
We feel corralled by common sense,
So up we jump, and leap the fence of reason!
We spoil the noblest possibilities
By taking them too far, too fast.
Anyway, that's how I see it.

ORGON. I bow to your superior knowledge.
You're the font of all wisdom,
You alone have got a brain – you're the oracle,
The greatest philosopher since the Greeks.
The rest of us are morons.

CLÉANTE. I'm no philosopher, I make no such claims;
I don't have special knowledge.
But I do see things for what they are,
I can tell truth from make-believe.
I yield to no one in my admiration
For true piety; there's nothing in the world
More noble or inspiring than passionate,
Genuine belief. But, what could be more vile
Than the various disguises
Charlatans use to hide their hypocrisy?
These paid-up wailers and gnashers of teeth,
Who demolish what others hold sacred,
Wreck people's lives and don't have to answer for it.
Money's their only religion;

The church is where they ply their trade;
They deal in beatific looks, eyes cast down
Or raised to Heaven, whichever pays best.
By helping God, they're lining their own pockets.
Clutching the Good Book,
They pray all the way to the bank.
They come back from parties at the palace
Preaching the pleasures of the simple life.
Vice and virtue are hand in glove for them;
They're spiteful, quick-tempered, cunning,
Liars through and through; and to ruin someone
They'll invoke the will of God.
What makes them doubly dangerous, though, when
    they're riled,
Is the way they use the weapons of religion
Against us; it's their zeal that makes them plunge
The sword of righteousness in our backs.
There's a lot of them about, but, thank Heaven,
The true believers aren't too hard to spot.
In recent years, there've been plenty
Who merit our admiration;
Look at Ariston, Périandre,
Oronte, Alcidamas, Polydore, Clitandre.
All of them devout and sincere,
As everyone agrees. They don't tell the world
How virtuous they are; they don't need
To trumpet the fact; they're sensible,
Reasonable human beings.
They don't go jumping down our throats
With 'Do this, don't do that!' No,
For them, actions speak louder than words;
They're no clanging empty kettles.

They refuse to point the finger of blame,
But rather see the good in people.
They steer well clear of cliques and intrigue,
And concentrate on living virtuously.
They don't condemn poor sinners –
That must wait till Judgement Day –
But keep their hate for sin itself.
That's true humility,
That's what we should seek to emulate.
Your man is of a different breed, Orgon.
It's not that I doubt your good faith;
But you're bewitched; you just can't see what's what.

ORGON. Finished?

CLÉANTE. Yes.

ORGON. Good day to you.

CLÉANTE. Alright, let's change the subject.
    You've promised Valère
    Your daughter's hand in marriage.

ORGON. Well?

CLÉANTE. And the date's been fixed.

ORGON. So?

CLÉANTE. Why put it off?

ORGON. Why not?

CLÉANTE. Have you got some other scheme?

ORGON. Who can say?

CLÉANTE. Have you changed your mind?

ORGON. Maybe.

CLÉANTE. Why the delay?
 Has something happened?

ORGON. Can't say.

CLÉANTE. I'll come to the point.
 Valère's asked me to see you.

ORGON. He has?

CLÉANTE. What shall I tell him?

ORGON. Tell him?

CLÉANTE. He needs to know what you intend to do.

ORGON. God's will.

CLÉANTE. Let's get this straight.
 Can Valère count on you, yes or no?

ORGON. Goodbye. (*Exits.*)

CLÉANTE. Things don't look good for Valère.
 He must be told what's going on.

ACT TWO

1. ORGON, MARIANE.

ORGON. Mariane.

MARIANE. Father?

ORGON. Come here, we need to have a little chat.

He looks behind a door.

MARIANE. Have you lost something?

ORGON. I'm checking
To see no one's listening,
It's the perfect place for spies . . .
Good, the coast is clear . . .
Mariane, my sweet girl,
You're my very favourite daughter.

MARIANE. Thank you, father.

ORGON. Now, a special little girl
Should want to please her old papa.

MARIANE. Oh yes, of course.

ORGON. Good, good . . . What do you think of Tartuffe?

MARIANE. Me?

ORGON. Yes . . . Off you go, then!

MARIANE. What would you like me to say?

ORGON. You might mention
That he's a man of integrity,
That you can't stop thinking about him,
That you're delighted I've chosen him
To be your husband . . . Eh?

MARIANE. Eh?

ORGON. Something wrong?

MARIANE. Excuse me?

ORGON. Well?

MARIANE. Did I hear right?

ORGON. What?

MARIANE. Who is it I'm supposed to say
I can't stop thinking about,
And you want me to marry?

ORGON. Tartuffe.

MARIANE. Father, is this a joke?
Why do you want me to tell lies?

ORGON. But I want it to be true.
That should be enough for you.

MARIANE. You seriously want . . . ?

ORGON. Yes. That way, I can make Tartuffe
A fully-fledged member of the family.
He will be your husband,
My mind's made up.
As for your wishes, I . . .

2. DORINE, ORGON, MARIANE.

ORGON. Have you come here to stick your nose
   Into other people's business?

DORINE. It may be my suspicious mind
   Or a bit of careless talk, but I've just heard
   Something about a marriage plan.
   I dismissed it – naturally.

ORGON. What do you mean, dismissed?

DORINE. Well, it's hogwash, Monsieur.

ORGON. No, it's true.

DORINE. And pigs might fly.

ORGON. You wait and see.

DORINE. Yeah, yeah.

ORGON. Mariane, I meant what I said.

DORINE. No he doesn't.
   He's gone mad.

ORGON. I tell you . . .

DORINE. Sorry, no one will believe it.

ORGON. I've had quite enough of you.

DORINE. Keep your hair on.
   How come, with that kind face
   And that lovely big beard,
   You can be so downright daft?

ORGON. You're treading on thin ice, Dorine.
   Who do you think you are?

DORINE. Let's stay calm, Monsieur, eh?
   You're insulting our intelligence,
   Giving your daughter to that bigot,
   Who should have higher things to think about.
   What would you gain from such a match?
   What motive could you possibly have,
   With all your wealth, to give her to a pauper?

ORGON. It's because he's poor
   That we should honour and respect him.
   His noble calling is poverty.
   He has no time for luxury;
   He's given everything he had away.
   This hollow world leaves him cold;
   He burns for the kingdom of Heaven.
   Nevertheless, with my help,
   He could at least get back that small estate
   He has a claim to – he's not what you think,
   You know; he's from the upper echelons.

DORINE. So he says; his snobbery
   Sits very badly with his 'piety'.
   Those who aspire to the virtuous life
   Should shut up about their lineage.
   There's no place for that kind of vanity
   For someone who's truly religious.
   Hasn't he heard of the sin of Pride? . . .
   This is getting nowhere. Forget *who* he is,
   Let's discuss *what* he's like. Wouldn't it bother you
   To foist that kind of man on your little girl?

It's not right. What would people say?
Have you thought through the consequences?
Don't you know that if a girl doesn't get
What she wants in a marriage, she'll rebel?
Staying faithful depends on what the husband's like.
Cuckolds bring it on themselves –
It's not the poor wife's fault.
Sometimes you can't blame her for straying,
When you see the specimen she's lumbered with.
Fathers who give their daughters to men they loathe
Must answer to God if they misbehave.
You should think again, Monsieur.

ORGON. I don't need your advice, thank you.

DORINE. I do know what I'm talking about.

ORGON. Mariane, pay no attention to this rubbish;
I'm your father, I know what you need.
Yes, I had promised you to Valère,
But I've heard he's fond of gambling,
And that he's an agnostic, maybe worse.
I've not seen him once in our church.

DORINE. You want him to rush in when he knows
You're there, like those who do it all for show?

ORGON. If I want your comments, I'll ask . . .
No one's closer to God than that man;
He's the greatest prize you'll ever have.
Marrying him will be pure bliss,
It will answer every prayer.
Two lives joined in mutual fidelity,
Like little children, like a pair of turtledoves!

There'll never be a cross word spoken;
He'll be all that you could want.

DORINE. Yes, a cuckold!

ORGON. Quiet!

DORINE. It's written all over him.
It's his destiny, and all your daughter's virtue
Won't change a thing.

ORGON. Not another word!

DORINE. I'm only thinking of you.

ORGON. No need, thanks very much.

She interrupts him every time he tries to address MARIANE.

DORINE. If we didn't love you . . .

ORGON. I don't want to be loved.

DORINE. But *I* want to, so there!

ORGON. Ah!

DORINE. I care about you. I can't bear it
That you're a universal laughing-stock.

ORGON. Will you shut up!

DORINE. I couldn't live with myself
If I let this marriage go ahead.

ORGON. That does it!

DORINE. Ahah! The man of peace!

ORGON. I'll burst a blood vessel
With all this nonsense.

DORINE. Alright . . . You can't stop me thinking, though.

ORGON. Go ahead, but keep it to yourself.
Not another squeak . . .
Mariane, I've given serious thought to . . .

DORINE. Arrrh! I'll explode!

She shuts up whenever he turns towards her.

ORGON. Tartuffe may be no Adonis . . .

DORINE. You said it!

ORGON. . . . And even if you're unimpressed
By his manifest qualities . . .

Turns towards DORINE, *arms folded.*

DORINE. She *still* should count herself fortunate! . . . Ha,
No man would marry *me* against my will
And live. He'd discover soon enough
That when a woman wants revenge . . .

ORGON. Didn't you hear me?

DORINE. What's the problem? I'm not speaking to you.

ORGON. Who to, then?

DORINE. Myself.

ORGON. Right. You've gone too far.
You need a damn good slap.

Raises hand to strike DORINE. *Whenever he looks her way,
she freezes into silence.*

Mariane, accept that the husband . . . I've chosen . . .
(*To* DORINE.) Why don't you speak?

ryone worships him anyway,
at with those looks, those red ears, that red face,
to mention that blue blood!
, you'll make the perfect couple.

IANE. Oh God!

INE. What a gorgeous creature!
e joy of being hitched to it!

IANE. You've made your point, Dorine.
give in. Do something.
ve me – please!

RINE. No, no, daughters obey their fathers.
he wants you to marry an ape,
hat's what you must do – and smile about it.
ou'll go for little drives around his little town,
all on his little relatives.
The smart set will invite you to their 'dos';
The Under Sheriff's wife and the Tax Inspector's
Good lady will be *très enchantées* for a week,
Then drop you. There'll be the annual parade,
The ball, the dance-band (well, two bagpipes
Sounding like a pair of strangled cats), plus
A puppet-show complete with performing monkey –
That is, if your husband . . .

ARIANE. Don't go on; help me!

ORINE. Sorry.

ARIANE. Please!

ORINE. You've made your bed . . .

DORINE. Nothing to say to myself.

ORGON. One word will do.

DORINE. Not in the mood.

ORGON. I'm waiting.

DORINE. And I'm not stupid.

ORGON. Mariane, I demand obedience
And complete submission.

DORINE (*running off*). I'd not marry him
If he was the last man on earth!

ORGON (*tries to strike her, misses*).
That busybody's got to be dismissed.
The insolence! If she stays on here,
I shan't answer for myself.
She'll give me an ulcer . . .
Let's stop this now, I need some air.

3. DORINE, MARIANE.

DORINE. Have you lost your tongue?
Must I do everything?
You let your father cook up crazy schemes,
And you just sit there like a stuffed doll.

MARIANE. What can I do? He's so pig-headed.

DORINE. Fight. Stand up to him.

MARIANE. How?

DORINE. He can't tell you who to love;
    It's *you* that's getting married, not him.
    Your husband's got to be to *your* liking,
    Not your father's.
    If he's so smitten with Tartuffe,
    He can marry him himself.

MARIANE. I couldn't speak like that to my father!

DORINE. Let's get this understood. Valère's declared his
    hand,
    He wants you – Do you want him?

MARIANE. That's so unfair, Dorine. Why are you against
    me?
    I've told you how I feel, a thousand times,
    You know I'm hopelessly in love with him.

DORINE. How can I be sure you're serious?
    Perhaps Valère means nothing to you.

MARIANE. You're so cruel. You know my feelings exactly.

DORINE. So you do love him, then?

MARIANE. Desperately.

DORINE. And he loves you?

MARIANE. I think so, yes.

DORINE. You both want to get married,
    More than anything else?

MARIANE. Oh yes.

DORINE. And your father's plan?

MARIANE. If it goes ahead, I'll kill myself.

DORINE. Bravo! I hadn't thought of that.
    Very neat and tidy, the perfect solution . . .
    That kind of talk makes me see red!

MARIANE. Don't be like that, Dorine!
    Can't you show a bit of sympathy?

DORINE. Not when I see you being so downrigh

MARIANE. I'm not, I'm . . . timid.

DORINE. Timid! This is love, for crying out loud!

MARIANE. I'm not timid when it comes to Valère
    But *he* should make the first move, not me.

DORINE. Look, it's scarcely Valère's fault
    That your father's barking mad
    And so besotted with Tartuffe
    That he's reneging on his promise.

MARIANE. I shouldn't seem too eager to reject Tart
    Should I? It would make my feelings for Valère
    Look too obvious. That would be a cheap thing to
    My father didn't bring me up
    To go around flaunting myself like some . . .

DORINE. Alright. Fine. Have it your way.
    Monsieur Tartuffe then. So be it. My mistake.
    Sorry. It's a fantastic match.
    You're quite right, he's not just anybody.
    Madame Tartuffe! A name to conjure with!
    It's got a real ring about it.
    You'll be the envy of the world.

MARIANE. What should I do?

DORINE. Lie in it.

MARIANE. You know what I want . . .

DORINE. Too late. It's got to be Tartuffe –
Such stuff as dreams are made on.

MARIANE. Dorine, I've always turned to you . . .

DORINE. No. You're going to be Tartuffified.

MARIANE. Very well. Be cruel if you want, but go.
Despair will be my comforter.
There's always *one* thing I can do.

She starts to leave.

DORINE. Now then, come here. I shan't be angry any more.
Friends?

MARIANE. I'm telling you, Dorine,
I'll kill myself. I mean it.

DORINE. There, there, shhh. We'll find a way.
But here's Valère.

4. VALÈRE, MARIANE, DORINE.

VALÈRE. I've just heard some charming news, Mariane.

MARIANE. What?

VALÈRE. You're marrying Tartuffe.

MARIANE. It's my father's wish.

VALÈRE. I see. Your father's . . .

MARIANE. Changed his mind.
  He told me just now.

VALÈRE. Is this some joke?

MARIANE. No. He's set on it.

VALÈRE. What about you?

MARIANE. I'm not sure.

VALÈRE. That's decisive . . . You're not sure.

MARIANE. No.

VALÈRE. No?

MARIANE. What should I do?

VALÈRE. Marry him.

MARIANE. I should?

VALÈRE. Of course.

MARIANE. Really?

VALÈRE. Really . . . It's an offer
  You can't possibly refuse.

MARIANE. Alright then, I will.

VALÈRE. I bet you can't wait.

MARIANE. You neither.

VALÈRE. I'm only saying what you want to hear.

MARIANE. I've heard, thank you.

DORINE (*aside*). This could be fun.

VALÈRE. I stupidly thought you loved me.
      I should have known that when . . .

MARIANE. You said I should marry
      Who my father chooses.
      I said, alright I will,
      Seeing as you want me to.
      There's nothing more to add.

VALÈRE. You're twisting my words;
      You'd already made your mind up about me.
      This Tartuffe story provides you with a cover,
      That's all.

MARIANE. Right.

VALÈRE. You've never loved me, admit it.

MARIANE. Think that, if you want.

VALÈRE. I *do* think. But two can play this game;
      I'll find pastures new, I have my admirers.

MARIANE. I'm sure. There's so much to admire.

VALÈRE. Not if I'm to go by you.
      But there *is* someone I know
      Who'll welcome me with open arms.
      She'll more than make up for what I'm losing.

MARIANE. Losing? Hardly. You'll get over it.

VALÈRE. I certainly hope so.
      It's not just my heart that's wounded,

It's my pride as well.
What weakness to show love
For someone who's abandoned you!
I've got some forgetting to do,
But if I don't succeed, *you'll* never know.

MARIANE. What strength of character.

VALÈRE. Lots of people would see it my way.
Am I supposed to go on and on
Loving you while you plan a life
With someone else?
Aren't I entitled to look elsewhere?

MARIANE. Absolutely. Go ahead. I can't wait.

VALÈRE. Really?

MARIANE. Really.

VALÈRE. That's plain enough.
Goodbye. If that's what you want . . .

Starts to leave, comes back.

MARIANE. Yes.

VALÈRE. Just remember:
You pushed me to it.

MARIANE. I will.

VALÈRE. This is *your* doing, not mine.

MARIANE. As you please.

VALÈRE. Fine.

MARIANE. Fine.

VALÈRE. You'll never see me again.

MARIANE. Right.

VALÈRE. Eh? (*Turning back, at the door.*)

MARIANE. What?

VALÈRE. Did you say something?

MARIANE. Not me.

VALÈRE. Right . . . right. Goodbye.

MARIANE. Goodbye.

DORINE. That's quite enough of this stupidity.
    Would you credit it? You're both off your heads,
    You really are. Valère, come here.

    Tries to grab his arm; VALÈRE pretends to resist.

VALÈRE. Why?

DORINE. Come here!

VALÈRE. No, it's what she wants. Don't try to stop me.

DORINE. Stay.

VALÈRE. You won't change my mind.

DORINE. Ah!

MARIANE. If the sight of me so upsets him,
    It's for me to leave.

DORINE (*lets go of* VALÈRE, *runs to* MARIANE).
    Her now . . . Where are you off to?

MARIANE. Let go of me.

DORINE. Here.

MARIANE. No, Dorine, it's pointless.

VALÈRE. She can't bear to be near me;
  She won't have to now. We're through.

DORINE (*lets go of* MARIANE, *runs to* VALÈRE).
  Over my dead body!
  Heel! – both of you,
  Or else it's *me* who'll leave!

  Drags them together.

VALÈRE. Why should I?

MARIANE. What do you want?

DORINE. To knock some sense into you.
  You belong together,
  So get off your stupid high horses.

VALÈRE. But you heard her.

DORINE. Is that a reason?

MARIANE. You heard the things he said?

DORINE. You need your heads examined.
  Valère – you're the only man in her life.
  Mariane – he wants you, no one else.
  Trust me.

MARIANE. What about his 'advice'?

VALÈRE. What about her 'suggestions'?

DORINE. Put a sock in it.
  Give me your hand, Valère. Come.

VALÈRE (*giving his hand to* DORINE). Why?

DORINE. Now yours, Mariane.

MARIANE (*giving her hand to* DORINE). What for?

DORINE. Stop these silly games!
  You're mad about each other,
  In case you didn't know.

VALÈRE (*to* MARIANE). Look as if you mean it. Try to
    smile.

  MARIANE *does*.

DORINE. Love! I ask you!

VALÈRE. I had every reason to complain.
  The things you said, they were meant to hurt!

MARIANE. I like that! Coming from you, that's rich!

DORINE. And they're off again! . . . Continue this
  Another time. We've got to do something
  About this crazy marriage plan.

MARIANE. What *can* we do?

DORINE. Lots. Your father's not serious underneath,
  His brains are boiled; he's temporarily deranged.
  You'd better go along with him,
  So that if it comes to the crunch,
  You can use delaying tactics
  Without arousing his suspicions.
  Play for time, that's our best chance;
  Plead a sudden illness needing lengthy treatment.
  Or say you've seen a dead body,

Or broken a mirror, or stepped in a puddle,
Any bad omen you can think of.
Keep this going, and there'll be no wedding;
You'll still be free to marry Valère.
But your father mustn't find you together.
(*To* VALÈRE.) You'd best leave. Talk to your friends,
Enlist their help. Meanwhile,
We'll recruit Monsieur Orgon's brother-in-law,
And Madame Elmire as well.
Now, off with you both. Shoo.

VALÈRE (*to* MARIANE). I'm not sure where this will get us.
But of one thing I *am* sure – you.

MARIANE (*to* VALÈRE). I can't answer for my father,
But you, I'll answer to for ever.

VALÈRE. Oh, how happy that makes me!
And whatever . . .

DORINE. Yack, yack, yack . . . Love! Go on!

VALÈRE (*moves away, then returns*). But if . . .

DORINE. Will you shut up? Get out!
(*Pushing each of them.*) You, this way. You, through there.

ACT THREE

1. DAMIS, DORINE.

DAMIS. May lightning strike me dead,
   May I be mocked and pilloried
   If I let anything or anyone
   Stop me from solving this crisis!

DORINE. Damis, calm down.
   Your father's scheme, it's early days.
   There's many a slip twixt cup and Tartuffe's lip.

DAMIS. That villain's wings are going to be clipped,
   And no mistake. Where is he?

DORINE. Don't start again! Let your stepmother
   Work on him, and on your father too.
   Tartuffe respects her; he's practically eating
   Out of her hand. I sometimes wonder
   If he's not completely smitten –
   Which could be very useful.
   She's sent for him, mainly on your account;
   She wants to know what he feels about
   This marriage plan, which spells bad news for you,
   And what dire consequences there'd be
   If he went along with it.
   I haven't been able to see him;
   His servant says he's at prayer,

But will be down at any moment.
Go now, let me deal with him.

DAMIS. I want to be present.

DORINE. No. He and Madame have to be alone.

DAMIS. I won't say a thing.

DORINE. Who are you kidding? We know what *that* means.
You'd ruin everything. Please, out!

DAMIS. I'm staying put. I promise to behave.

DORINE. Look Damis, I've said . . .
He's here. Quick, hide!

DAMIS *hides in a cubby-hole upstage.*

2. TARTUFFE, LAURENT, DORINE.

TARTUFFE (*seeing* DORINE). Laurent, put my hair-shirt and
my scourge away,
And pray for God's guidance every hour.
If I'm wanted, say I've gone to offer
My last few coins to the inmates of the prison.

DORINE (*aside*). Vintage Tartuffe!

TARTUFFE. What do you want?

DORINE. I've got a message from . . .

TARTUFFE (*producing his handkerchief*).
Ah, please, before you go on,
Take this.

DORINE. What?

TARTUFFE. Cover that bosom I'm not meant to see.
　　Things like that attack the soul,
　　And stir up wicked thoughts.

DORINE. You're easily aroused . . .
　　The sight of flesh too much for you?
　　I don't know what your trouble is,
　　But one thing I can say: you could be standing there
　　Stark naked, head to toe, and nothing I might see
　　Could ever blow my frock up.

TARTUFFE. Kindly moderate your language,
　　Or I shall have to withdraw.

DORINE. Alright, I'll leave you in peace.
　　But a quick word first; Madame
　　Will be down in a minute or two.
　　She'd appreciate a little of your time.

TARTUFFE. I'd be delighted.

DORINE (*aside*). I bet he would! Look at him,
　　Wobbling with anticipation.

TARTUFFE. Will she be long?

DORINE. That's her now . . .
　　I'll leave you to it.

3. ELMIRE, TARTUFFE.

TARTUFFE. May God in His infinite goodness
   Preserve you in body and soul;
   May He grant you all the joy that I,
   His humble servant, also wish for you.

ELMIRE. Thank you for those kind thoughts.

   Indicating a chair.

   Shall we make ourselves more comfortable.

TARTUFFE. Are you feeling any better?

ELMIRE. Much, thank you.

TARTUFFE. My humble prayers, I'm afraid,
   Won't have done all I'd have wished
   To obtain this happy outcome; please know
   That I prayed for you day and night.

ELMIRE. You shouldn't have.

TARTUFFE. Nothing's more dear to me than your health.
   If it could help, I'd gladly give you mine.

ELMIRE. Very Christian, I'm sure,
   But thank you, no.

TARTUFFE. I'd love to help you more.

ELMIRE. I wanted a word with you in private.
   Now's a good time; no one's around.

TARTUFFE. I too am glad that we're alone.
   It's what I've hoped and prayed for,
   And now – at last – God has heard me.

ELMIRE. May we be frank?
Shall we lay our cards on the table?

TARTUFFE. The one favour I ask Heaven
Is to let me bare my heart to you.
Please believe that the objections I've raised
About the visitors you attract here
Were not made in any spirit of rage or scorn,
But rather by a pure, intense concern
For the state of . . .

ELMIRE. My soul, I know.

TARTUFFE (*squeezing her fingertips*). Indeed, yes. So intense
that . . .

ELMIRE. Ouch!

TARTUFFE. A thousand pardons!
I would never hurt you.

Putting his hand on her knee.

It's my deep interest in . . .

ELMIRE. What's that doing there?

TARTUFFE. Feeling the fabric. Isn't it soft!

ELMIRE. Please don't, I'm ticklish.

She edges her chair away; he edges his closer.

TARTUFFE (*fiddling with her shawl*).
Heavens, what fabulous lace!
The miracles they do these days!
I've never seen such fine work.

ELMIRE. Can we get to the point?
  It seems my husband's going back on his word,
  And now wants *you* for his son-in-law.
  Am I wrong?

TARTUFFE. He has mentioned it, although, to be honest,
  That's not the happiness I long for. No,
  The perfect ecstasy I crave lies somewhere else.

ELMIRE. You mean, life everlasting?

TARTUFFE. I had in mind the here-and-now.

ELMIRE. You surprise me. I'd assumed
  You rose above our world of imperfection.

TARTUFFE. Heavenly beauty and one more down-to-earth
  Aren't mutually exclusive. One can love both,
  Since God made both. Their perfections
  Quite devastate the senses.
  Ethereal beauty's reflected in your own,
  Madame, as though you'd been sent from Heaven,
  And God had concentrated His greatest beauties
  In your divine and wonderful face.
  Whenever I behold you, perfect creature,
  I see the Maker I worship.
  My heart swells with love, gazing
  Upon God's perfect self-portrait.
  At first, I was fearful that this secret glow
  Was the Devil trying to trip me up.
  I resolved to keep away from you,
  Worried you might lead me down the slippery slope.
  But eventually I saw that the fires
  Your beauty lit in me needn't pose

Any problems of theology.
Forgive my audacity, Madame,
But I'm yours for you to take.
Perhaps you'll find it in your heart
To pardon me my weakness – God knows, I've struggled!
In you lie my hope, my future, my peace of mind.
Only you can pass sentence on this anguished soul.
Decide, give me your verdict. Either
Take me to Heaven or damn me to perdition.

ELMIRE. Your declaration's very flattering,
    But, I have to say, surprising too.
    In your shoes, I'd have been much firmer
    With myself, made myself see sense.
    For someone known round here for his spiritual . . .

TARTUFFE. I may be spiritual, but I'm still a man!
    (*His hand on his heart.*) When one sees your splendours,
    It hits home, like the sweetest arrow;
    Reason flies out of the window.
    Yes, Madame, this may sound odd,
    But I'm no angel, after all.
    If you find me reprehensible,
    Blame it on your charms.
    The first time I saw you,
    I fell hopelessly under their spell.
    Your Heavenly eyes melted the resistance
    My stubborn heart was putting up.
    I prayed, I wept, I fasted – to no avail.
    I was drawn in more and more. But you know this;
    You've seen how I look at you and sigh . . .
    Yes, I'll put my cards on the table:
    Can't you look kindly on this wretch?

Can't you find it in your heart
To pour the balm of consolation
On your unworthy slave
Writhing in agony here at your feet?
Oh, you creature from Heaven,
Be the temple where I worship!
I can guarantee complete discretion;
You'd have nothing to fear on my account.
Your honour's safe with me, not like those loud-mouths
At court, and their stupid wives, who shout
Their every exploit from the rooftops.
They don't care what they say, or to whom.
They violate the altar of their sacrifice.
But people like us are different; passion burns
Under cover, hidden from view.
By watching our own reputations,
We safeguard the lady's good name.
Those who accept our offer enjoy
Love without scandal, pleasure without fear.

ELMIRE. That was quite a speech. Your language
Leaves no room for ambiguity.
Hasn't it occurred to you that I might tell
My husband what you really want?
This sudden revelation
Could change his opinion of you.

TARTUFFE. I know you wouldn't be that cruel.
I'm sure you'll forgive my forwardness,
And the human weakness that fans the flames
Of a violent love you seem to be rejecting.
Please, look in the mirror, see what I see;
You mustn't forget that men are made of flesh.

ELMIRE. Not everyone would, but I shall be discreet;
    I shan't say a word to my husband.
    However, I want something in return:
    Valère, Mariane, their marriage –
    You must do all you can to make it happen.
    You must relinquish all claims
    Which by rights belong to someone else,
    And . . .

4. DAMIS, ELMIRE, TARTUFFE.

DAMIS (*emerging from his hiding-place*).
    No! This must be made public.
    I was in there, thank God, I heard everything.
    Now I can expose the traitor.
    He won't harm me any longer.
    Revenge, at last, we've got him!
    No more of his shameless hypocrisy!
    I'll open my father's eyes, denounce this pervert,
    This lecher with only one thing on his mind!

ELMIRE. No, Damis, this need go no further; let Tartuffe
    Mend his ways and try to merit our forgiveness.
    I've made a promise I must stick by.
    I don't want any fuss
    Over something so petty.
    There's no need to tell my husband.

DAMIS. You do it your way, if you want,
    I'll do it mine. It would be an outrage
    To let him off the hook.

Too long I've kept quiet about the fact
That the mealy-mouthed monster's destroying us.
No wonder I'm angry.
My father does exactly what 'Monsieur' says.
'Monsieur' is out to wreck Valère's happiness,
And mine too, or didn't you know?
Father must be made to see sense.
Here's a golden opportunity, thank God,
And we'd be mad not to seize it.

ELMIRE. Damis . . .

DAMIS. Please, don't obstruct me,
    Don't try to talk me round.
    Nothing you say will deflect me
    From the path of sweet revenge,
    And that's final.
    (*Spotting* ORGON.) Ah, the very person . . .

5. ORGON, DAMIS, TARTUFFE, ELMIRE.

DAMIS. You've come at just the right moment. Listen to this.
    Your Monsieur Tartuffe, who's been happy to accept
    Your kindness, now returns the compliment
    By dishonouring you – he calls it loyalty.
    I've caught him red-handed
    Propositioning your wife,
    But she wanted to hush it up; that's her style,
    But it's not mine. Treachery on that scale
    Can't be left unpunished. You had to know.

ELMIRE. I don't think husbands should be troubled
    By things as slight as this.
    Honour scarcely enters into it;
    Wives must learn to cope with . . . situations.
    That's my opinion, anyway.
    And if I had any influence over you,
    Damis, you'd have kept your big mouth shut.

6. ORGON, DAMIS, TARTUFFE.

ORGON. What am I hearing?
    Can it be true, dear God in Heaven?

TARTUFFE. Yes, brother, I am evil, guilty,
    A miserable sinner, full of iniquity,
    The vilest wretch that ever trod this earth;
    Every second of my criminal life
    Is steeped in filth; I'm a stinking cesspool;
    Now God wants to mortify me –
    I deserve the punishment.
    Whatever I'm accused of
    I shan't have the gall to deny.
    Believe what you're told; get angry,
    Send me packing like a common thief.
    Pile shame on me as high as you can,
    And when you've finished, start again.

ORGON (to DAMIS). Traitor! How dare you besmirch this
    pure man's name
    With your odious, disgusting lies?

DAMIS. What? What?? Don't you see what his game is?
    The man's a total hypocrite!

ORGON. Damn you, damn your eyes!

TARTUFFE. No, you're wrong to blame him. Let him speak.
    Hear him out, believe what he says.
    Why take my side? After all,
    You don't know what I'm capable of.
    Don't go by appearances.
    Because I seem virtuous, you think me better
    Than I am. But no, I'm exactly
    What people take me for. In fact, I'm worse.
    The plain truth is, I'm the most awful man alive.
    (*To* DAMIS.) Yes, dear boy, speak out, call me traitor,
    Lost cause, rogue, murderer, thief,
    And more, anything you can think of.
    I accept it all, it's what I deserve.
    I want to crawl through the world on my knees,
    Weighed down by my shameful crimes.

ORGON (*to* TARTUFFE). Oh, my brother, please, no more!
    (*To* DAMIS.) Is your heart made of stone?

DAMIS. Can't you see through this rubbish?

ORGON (*to* DAMIS). Quiet!
    (*To* TARTUFFE.) Please, get up!
    (*To* DAMIS.) Words fail me!

DAMIS. He . . .

ORGON. Shut up!

DAMIS. I can't believe this! I try . . .

ORGON. Say another word, and I'll break your arms!

TARTUFFE. In the name of God, brother, peace!
  I'd rather suffer the direst pain
  Than let you harm a hair of his head.

ORGON (*to* DAMIS). You hear that?

TARTUFFE. I beg of you, forgive him.
  Look, on my knees, I implore you . . .

ORGON (*also dropping to his knees, addressing* TARTUFFE).
  It's not possible!
  (*To* DAMIS.) You see how good he is?

DAMIS. So . . .

ORGON. Stop!

DAMIS. Don't you . . . ?

ORGON. Enough. I know full well why you hate him.
  Everybody does, my wife, my children,
  My servants, all conspiring to bring him down.
  You're using every shabby trick to chase
  This paragon of virtue from my house.
  But the more you try, the more I'll dig in.
  I'm giving him to my daughter –
  And serve everyone right!

DAMIS. You'll force her to marry him?

ORGON. Yes, today, for maximum annoyance.
  I defy the lot of you.
  Just remember who's in charge here.
  Take back your slanders, get down on your knees,
  And beg his forgiveness. Now!

DAMIS. Who, me? Ask this charlatan for his , . . ?

ORGON. You take that word back, you piece of filth!
(*To* TARTUFFE.) Fetch me a stick! No, don't try to stop me!
(*To* DAMIS.) Go, this instant, and never come back!

DAMIS. Alright, but . . .

ORGON. Out! I'm disinheriting you.
You'll get nothing from me now
Except my everlasting curse.

7. ORGON, TARTUFFE.

ORGON. Blasphemy! How dare that boy . . .

TARTUFFE.
Forgive him, Lord, for he knows not what he does!
(*To* ORGON.) Ah, the pain I suffer
When people try to blacken my name
And make you think . . .

ORGON. It's a cross we must bear!

TARTUFFE. The thought of such ingratitude
Is torment to my soul . . .
The horror . . . I'm too choked to speak.
I want to die.

ORGON (*in tears, running to the door which* DAMIS *left by*).
Wretch! I'm sorry I showed you mercy,
I should have killed you!
(*To* TARTUFFE.) There, there, brother, don't upset yourself.

TARTUFFE. Let's stop this. It's futile.
   I see the trouble I'm causing.
   I think it's high time I left.

ORGON. You're not serious, are you?

TARTUFFE. They're so full of hate. They want you to doubt
   me.

ORGON. I'll take no notice.

TARTUFFE. They won't give up, I know they won't.
   You may not listen to them now,
   But in a week, a month, a year?

ORGON. Never!

TARTUFFE. Ah, brother, your wife . . . Wives
   Can make husbands believe anything they want.

ORGON. No, no.

TARTUFFE. If I leave now, their attacks will cease.

ORGON. No, you're going to stay.
   Nothing matters more to me.

TARTUFFE. If you insist; it's the sacrifice
   God wants me to make. On the other hand . . .

ORGON. Ah!

TARTUFFE. We'll close the subject.
   But I know how I must act from now on.
   Your good name's at stake, and, as friends,
   There should be no mistrust between the two of us.
   Therefore, I'll steer clear of your wife, and . . .

ORGON. Absolutely not! Quite the reverse.
I love to irritate them all,
I want you to be seen with her round the clock.
And – my masterstroke –
I shall make my entire estate over to you;
The deeds will be put in your name today,
My good, true friend, my son-in-law!
What do I care for cousins, children, wives?
There, what do you say to that?

TARTUFFE. Amen.

ORGON. Poor man! Come on, there are papers to sign.
I want to watch this household die of envy!

ACT FOUR

1. CLÉANTE, TARTUFFE.

CLÉANTE. The whole place is buzzing, and I have to say
  You don't have very many allies.
  Still, I'm glad to have this chance, Monsieur,
  To share my views with you.
  There's no point raking up the muck;
  What's happened has happened.
  For argument's sake,
  Let's say Damis behaved badly,
  And that you've been falsely accused.
  The Christian way is to forgive,
  And put aside all thoughts of retribution.
  Should a private quarrel cause a father
  To banish his son from the house?
  Let me repeat – all kinds of people
  Are shocked. You should back off, call it a day;
  Offer your anger to God instead,
  Let father and son be reconciled.

TARTUFFE. I only wish I could!
  I feel, Monsieur, no bitterness, no blame;
  I forgive Damis everything.
  I'd do all in my power to help him.
  But Heaven ordains it otherwise,
  And if the boy returns, I go.
  After his scurrilous slanders,

Any link between us might smell bad.
What would people think? No doubt they'd say
I had ulterior motives,
That knowing I'm the guilty party,
I'm wheedling my way back in
To try to buy his silence.

CLÉANTE. Codswallop!
I've never heard anything so far-fetched!
You can't do God's work for Him;
He'll decide what punishment to give.
'Forgive us our trespasses', after all,
'As we forgive those who trespass against us.'
Leave it to God, and bow to His will.
You'd let a squalid fear of idle tongues
Stop you from doing this one act of charity?
No: we should do what God ordains,
And not be swayed by other matters.

TARTUFFE. I've said I forgive him in my heart,
As Heaven decrees. But after today's outburst,
It's *not* God's wish that I continue to live
Under the same roof as him.

CLÉANTE. And does God wish, Monsieur, that you indulge
His father's mad caprice?
Does Heaven say you must accept
An inheritance you're not entitled to?

TARTUFFE. Anyone who knows me well knows
That I do nothing for personal gain.
I care little for the trappings of this world;
All that glitters is false gold.
If – most reluctantly – I've accepted

What Monsieur Orgon's giving me,
It's only that I don't want to see it
Fall into the wrong hands.
Who knows what evil uses weaker men
Might put it to? Not to the glory of God,
Or our fellow creatures, as I intend.

CLÉANTE. These subtleties, Monsieur, won't impress
The rightful heir. He'll take you to court.
Why allow such matters to concern you?
Let Damis inherit – after that,
He's on his own. Better he should waste the lot
Than you be accused of purloining it.
I'm simply astonished that when the idea
Was put to you, you went along with it.
Name me the Gospel which says that rightful heirs
Can be disinherited on a whim.
And if Heaven's really saying
That you can't live in the same house as Damis,
Then *you* should have the grace to withdraw,
Rather than see that boy thrown out.
Believe me, as a token of good faith, it would . . .

TARTUFFE. It's half-past three, Monsieur, and time for
prayers.
I must go up. Excuse me.

2. ELMIRE, MARIANE, CLÉANTE, DORINE

DORINE. Monsieur Cléante, please help us!
   Poor Mariane's in total despair
   Because her father's decided
   To carry out his crazy plan – tonight!
   He's coming now. We must stop this madness,
   By guile or brute force, whichever . . .

3. ORGON, ELMIRE, MARIANE, CLÉANTE, DORINE.

ORGON. Ah, good, everyone's here.
   (*To* MARIANE.) Look, the contract which will seal your
   happiness;
   You know what it contains.

MARIANE (*on her knees*).
   Father, in the name of Heaven, in the name
   Of everything that's dear to you,
   Release me from a daughter's obligation.
   Don't make me give up what I've set my heart on,
   Don't make me wish I'd never been born – please!
   But if you're determined to ruin my hopes
   Of happiness with the man I love,
   At least, I implore you, don't make my life
   A living Hell, don't make me do something drastic
   Which you'd only regret.

ORGON (*feeling himself melting*).
   Stay firm, my heart, no human weakness now!

MARIANE. You can cherish that man as much as you like,
    It doesn't matter to me. Give him all your wealth;
    And if you want more, give him my share too;
    You're welcome to it, it's all yours, have it.
    Give him anything except me. Let me hang on
    To myself, let me spend the rest of my sad life
    In some forgotten convent.

ORGON. The female heart! Thwarted in love,
    They rush off and take the veil! . . . Get up!
    The more you kick against Tartuffe,
    The stronger you'll become; it's good for your soul.
    This will be a marriage to mortify the flesh . . .
    And now, let's change the subject; my head's hurting.

DORINE. You mean to . . .

ORGON. You, keep your nose out of what doesn't concern
    you.

CLÉANTE. If I might give you some advice . . .

ORGON. I've no doubt yours is the best,
    Thoughtful and considered. Usually I heed it,
    But not today, thank you.

ELMIRE (*to* ORGON). You leave me speechless.
    How can anyone be so blind?
    Are you that besotted
    You can't see what's going on?

ORGON. I see what I see.
    You and my worthless son are thick as thieves,
    Which explains why you wouldn't disown him
    When he attacked my poor Tartuffe.

You were far too calm to be believed –
It might have been different if you'd been distraught.

ELMIRE. A man tells a woman he admires her,
And she's got to scream blue murder?
You wanted fiery words and flashing eyes?
Well no, that method's too flamboyant,
And in the end pathetic.
Softly softly is the best approach.
I've no time for hatchet-wielding witches,
The self-appointed defenders of honour
Who scratch out men's eyes if they so much as look
In their direction. If that's the new morality,
God help us! Virtue has no need of bully-girls;
I believe the cold shoulder, elegantly turned,
Will freeze any man in his tracks.

ORGON. I know what I know, I can see straight.

ELMIRE. You've got such a blind spot, it beggars belief.
Shall we show you what's really going on,
Make you understand, once and for all?

ORGON. Show me?

ELMIRE. Yes.

ORGON. Don't be silly.

ELMIRE. Here, now, before your very eyes?

ORGON. Absurd.

ELMIRE. What a man!
Don't just take our word for it;
If we found you a hiding place

So you could overhear everything,
What would you say about your saint then?

ORGON. In that case, I'd say . . . I'd say nothing,
Because it's not possible.

ELMIRE. This farce has gone on long enough.
I'm tired of being thought a liar.
You'll have to learn the hard way.

ORGON. Right, agreed. Since you're making such rash
    promises,
Let's see you try to keep them.

ELMIRE (*to* DORINE). Bring him here.

DORINE. Don't you think he'll smell a rat? He's no fool.

ELMIRE. No, but he's blinkered by love and conceit.
It often happens. Fetch him now, Dorine.
(*To* CLÉANTE *and* MARIANE.) You two, go.

4. ELMIRE, ORGON.

ELMIRE. Help me with this table . . . Now, get under.

ORGON. What?

ELMIRE. You must hide.

ORGON. Under the table?

ELMIRE. Don't argue, I know what I'm doing. Trust me!
And make sure you can't be seen or heard.

ORGON. The things I have to do! . . .
   It had better be worth it.

ELMIRE. You'll thank me.

   ORGON *is now under the table*.

What happens next may startle you.
Try not to be shocked; read between the lines.
I want to convince you, that's all there is to it.
Since there's no alternative, I'll lead him on,
I'll tease and cajole him, lure him
Into taking risks, make him drop his mask
So you can see the hypocrite for what he is.
I'm going to pretend I've fallen for him,
But you must stop me when you've heard enough.
Things need go no further than you choose;
You can call a halt to his advances
The moment you *are* convinced.
Open your eyes, spare me further embarrassment,
Expose me only to the minimum.
It's up to you – decide . . .
Here he is. Keep out of sight, not a sound.

5. TARTUFFE, ELMIRE, ORGON.

TARTUFFE. You wanted to see me?

ELMIRE. Yes. There are . . . private things I want to say.
   But, please, close the door first,
   And have a good look round – we don't want interruptions.

TARTUFFE *closes the door; returns.*

The last thing we want is any reputation
Of what happened earlier.
I've not had such a fright in all my life.
Damis's antics made me fear for you.
You saw me do my level best
To calm him down, and spoil his plans.
I know, I didn't contradict him –
But I couldn't think straight. Anyway,
Thank the Lord, it's worked out for the best.
Crisis over! Your reputation did the trick.
My husband reproaches you nothing. In fact,
To defy malicious gossip, he's decided
That from now on, you and I should always be
Together, inseparable . . . That's why I'm here,
Alone with you, door locked,
Free of all possible blame,
Burning to bare my heart,
Aching for you to disclose
What it is that you're proposing.

TARTUFFE. I find your language troubling, Madame.
It was very different a short while ago.

ELMIRE. Ah, how little you know about our sex!
When a woman says no . . .
When she says it without much conviction,
It can mean something else.
In such circumstances, modesty
Fights against more pressing desires.
Love may make us glow inside,
But we still blush to declare it.

We put up resistance, as honour demands,
But soon we give in; we can't keep up the show
For long. Our lips may say one thing,
But inside, different things are bursting to come out . . .
Am I being too open? Perhaps I'm unwise
To confess these feminine secrets,
But now the cat's out of the bag, tell me,
Would I have wanted to restrain Damis,
Would I have listened to your declaration,
Would I have reacted the way I did
If your proposition hadn't pleased me?
And when I urged you to turn down
My husband's marriage plan,
Couldn't you read my coded message?
I was saying your attentions please me,
I was saying I'm jealous of having to share
Something I want all to myself.

TARTUFFE. It's the greatest pleasure in the world
To hear such words from the person one loves;
They're like sweet tongues of honey
Licking round one's body.
More than anything I want to please you;
Your happiness is my heart's ecstasy.
But my heart has to entertain some doubts
About the precise nature of its joy.
Maybe your words are calculated *only*
To make me refuse this impending marriage.
Let's be clear we understand each other;
I shan't trust your teasing words unless and until
You match them with some actions of the kind
I long for. My soul needs something to get hold of,

Some tangible evidence, a little taste
Of the charms you have in store for me.

ELMIRE (*coughing to alert* ORGON).
You don't waste much time, do you?
Women like to be won over slowly.
It wasn't easy to declare my feelings,
But here you are, wanting more, immediately.
Will you only be satisfied
If I yield to you entirely?

TARTUFFE. The less one deserves, the less one dares expect.
Words are cheap; it's deeds that count.
One can't trust the promise of pleasures to come;
They must be had if they're to be believed.
I'm so unsure of you; I wonder what
My reckless advances have really achieved.
The truth is, Madame, I shan't be convinced
Until you've turned fiction into fact.

ELMIRE. You're making me giddy. Your love's all teeth and
claws.
It's like a beast that's got me by the neck,
And is shaking me to death!
Please, slow down a bit, let me catch my breath!
I can't think straight. Surely it's not right to insist
On instant gratification?
It's taking advantage of someone
Who's already gone further than she ought.

TARTUFFE. But if you're well disposed towards me,
Why wait?

ELMIRE. How can I say yes without offending God?
You say you care so much about Him.

TARTUFFE. Oh, if that's what's stopping you,
    God's a hurdle we can easily jump.
    He needn't stand in our way.

ELMIRE. What about the Ten Commandments?

TARTUFFE. The fears you have are inappropriate,
    Madame; scruples can be got rid of.
    Yes, God's against certain pleasures;
    (*Molière's note here: 'It's a scoundrel speaking.'*)
    But He's open to persuasion.
    Things are never black and white; the rules of conscience
    Are elastic. There's an established way
    Of squaring bad actions with good intentions.
    I'll teach you the theology.
    Just place yourself in my hands,
    Give me what I want, and don't be scared. I'll take care
    Of everything; just leave the sin to me.

ELMIRE *coughs more loudly*.

That's a bad cough, Madame.

ELMIRE. Yes, it's too much.

TARTUFFE (*offering her something wrapped in paper*).
    Here, some liquorice will soothe it.

ELMIRE. My cold is very stubborn.
    All the liquorice in the world won't shift it.

TARTUFFE. That's a shame.

ELMIRE. Indeed!

TARTUFFE. As I was saying: forget your qualms.
    Total secrecy is guaranteed.

Sin happens only when things leak out,
That's when the problems start.
But to sin in silence doesn't count.

ELMIRE (*coughs again*). It seems I have no choice but to give in,
And grant you whatever you want;
Anything less won't be proper evidence.
I didn't want it this way;
It goes against my better judgement,
But, since I have no other choice,
Since more convincing proof is wanted
Before there's general satisfaction,
I must take the plunge.
If what happens now is wrong,
So much the worse for him who's forced the issue.
On his head be it.

TARTUFFE. That head, Madame, will happily bear . . .

ELMIRE. Would you go and make sure
My husband's not out there?

TARTUFFE. You needn't worry on *his* score.
He's a man one can lead by the nose.
He's even pleased he's brought us together!
There's none so blind as those who will not see.

ELMIRE. I'd still like you to go and do a thorough check.

6. ORGON, ELMIRE.

ORGON (*emerging from under the table*). What an abomination!
   I'm stunned, I can't believe it!

ELMIRE. Hello! You out so soon? Relax,
   Get back under, the best is yet to come!
   Don't jump to conclusions, wait till we're through;
   You mustn't let your imagination
   Run away with you.

ORGON. What pit of Hell did he crawl out of?

ELMIRE. You're being too hasty.
   Weigh the evidence nice and slowly.
   Take your time; I want you to be quite certain.

7. TARTUFFE, ELMIRE, ORGON.

TARTUFFE (*does not see* ORGON).
   Heaven is smiling on me, Madame.
   I've looked in all the rooms,
   There's no one about. The bliss which my soul . . .

ORGON (*appearing*). Stop right there, man of God!
   Your soul! You keep it in your trousers!
   Marry my daughter *and* seduce my wife?!
   You thought I wouldn't notice.
   I was biding my time, to give you
   The benefit of the doubt. But the more you said,
   The worse it got. So now, enough's enough. That's it.

ELMIRE (*to* TARTUFFE). I'm not proud of my part in this,
  Or the way I've treated you. But my hand was forced.

TARTUFFE. What? You really think . . .

ORGON. No arguments, no fuss.

TARTUFFE. My intention . . .

ORGON. Not another word. Out.
  You have ten seconds.

TARTUFFE. No, it's for *you* to leave, you who claim
  You're master of this house. You're not, *I* am,
  Understand? You'll soon see
  Your pathetic tricks can't touch me.
  You'll find out who you're dealing with.
  I know exactly how to bring down hypocrites,
  And punish impostors. I'll avenge
  Poor, suffering Heaven. You'll rue the day
  You thought you could expel Tartuffe!

8. ELMIRE, ORGON.

ELMIRE. What did he mean?

ORGON. Oh God, this is bad, this is very bad!

ELMIRE. What's happened?

ORGON. I've done a dreadful thing.
  A deed of gift, I've given him my whole estate!

ELMIRE. You've done what?

ORGON. I'm afraid it's signed and sealed.
　　But there's something even worse . . .

ELMIRE. Worse?

ORGON. I'll tell you later. Quick, my room.
　　Pray God a certain strong-box is still there.

ACT FIVE

1. ORGON, CLÉANTE.

CLÉANTE. Where are you running to?

ORGON. I don't know!

CLÉANTE. Let's sit down, and think what to do.

ORGON. That missing box is a catastrophe.

CLÉANTE. Why?

ORGON. My poor friend Argas gave it me
For safe keeping before he fled.
He swore me to secrecy,
Telling me it contained papers
Which his finances – no, his *life* – depended on.

CLÉANTE. Why did you entrust the box to someone else?

ORGON. A matter of conscience.
I told Tartuffe the whole story;
He persuaded me to give *him* the box,
So that, if the authorities launched a search,
I could truthfully say that I hadn't got it.

CLÉANTE. This does look very bad. The deed of gift,
The strong-box – most impetuous.
You could be in deep water, now that man
Has got the upper hand.

You were rash to tackle him head on;
More roundabout methods were needed.

ORGON. With someone who can hide that much evil
And duplicity under such a cloak
Of piety? . . . He had nothing; a beggar,
When I took him in! Well, men of God,
I spit on the lot of you! From now on,
You'll have *me* to reckon with!

CLÉANTE. There you go again;
Never anything in moderation;
From one extreme to the other,
Swinging like a manic pendulum.
You've acknowledged you were fooled
By a show of phoney zeal.
But two wrongs don't make a right.
There's no virtue now in going round
Finding rogues and impostors at every turn.
Because there's one rotten apple,
You think the barrel's full of scheming hypocrites.
Genuine believers *do* exist.
Leave cynicism to religious sceptics,
Learn to distinguish between virtue,
Real and feigned. Don't rush to instant judgement,
Try to keep a sense of balance.
Yes, treat hypocrisy as such,
But recognise sincere devotion.
And if you *have* to go to one extreme,
Trust people more, rather than less.

2. DAMIS, ORGON, CLÉANTE.

DAMIS. Father, is it really true
    That the wretch is issuing threats?
    Has he forgotten all you've done for him?
    Is your very kindness to be your downfall?

ORGON. Yes, Damis, this is the worst day of my life.

DAMIS. He won't get away with it!
    Don't worry, I'll see that he doesn't,
    Even if it means getting physical.
    Leave it to me!

CLÉANTE. There speaks the voice of youth . . .
    Show some restraint, if you please.
    We live in a civilised age
    Where nothing is solved by violence.

3. MADAME PERNELLE, MARIANE, ELMIRE, DORINE, DAMIS, ORGON, CLÉANTE.

MME. PERNELLE. I've been hearing dreadful things.

ORGON. All true, mother, as I can vouch.
    I feed and shelter a destitute man,
    Treat him like a brother,
    Shower him with favours, give him all my wealth,
    And my daughter's hand; meanwhile,
    The villain's seducing my wife!
    Not content with that, he calmly turns

My good deeds into weapons to use against me.
This is the thanks I get . . .
I've been so stupid! He's going to evict us
From our house – no, *his*! He'll reduce us
To the very state I found him in.

DORINE. Poor man!

MME. PERNELLE. Son, I can't believe he's as black as you
    paint him.

ORGON. What?

MME. PERNELLE. Good people are always easy targets.

ORGON. Have you taken leave of your senses?

MME. PERNELLE. Funny things go on in this house.
    And it's no secret how much Tartuffe is loathed.

ORGON. What's that got to do with it?

MME. PERNELLE. I used to tell you this when you were
    small:
    'Virtue's what we seek to know;
    The envious die, but envy, no.'

ORGON. I don't see the connection.

MME. PERNELLE. The stories about him are fabrications.

ORGON. But I *saw.*

MME. PERNELLE. Appearances are deceptive.

ORGON. Don't provoke me, mother.
    I tell you, I saw it with my own eyes.

MME. PERNELLE. You've been poisoned by vitriolic gossip.

ORGON. You need your head looked at, mother, frankly.
    How many more times? Shall I shout it?
    I saw – with these two things called eyes.
    Subject: *I*, verb: *saw*!

MME. PERNELLE. The eye plays tricks.
    You've got to look below the surface.

ORGON. I'll go mad!

MME. PERNELLE. It's a common failing to think the
    worst.
    White is often seen as black.

ORGON. Wanting to make love to my wife
    Was an act of selfless charity?

MME. PERNELLE. Don't make accusations
    Without first checking your facts.

ORGON. I see. Concrete proof. Silly me,
    I should have awaited developments,
    Watched him un- . . . Do you really want me to go on?

MME. PERNELLE. He's on a far too lofty plane
    To do anything like that.
    It's just not possible.

ORGON. I'm speechless. If you weren't my mother . . .

DORINE (*to* ORGON). Poetic justice, Monsieur.
    You wouldn't believe *us*, she won't believe *you*.

CLÉANTE. We're wasting valuable time;
    We need a strategy
    To stop Tartuffe from going any further.

DAMIS. You think he'll try?

ELMIRE. Surely he wouldn't dare?
   He knows he'd be unmasked.

CLÉANTE. I wouldn't be so certain. He'll find ways
   Of making you the guilty party.
   There are powerful cabals and cliques out there;
   Unsuspecting people have suffered worse than this
   At their hands, and for less.
   No, with the weapons Tartuffe's got,
   You shouldn't have pushed him so far.

ORGON. What else could I do? He was so brazen.
   I lost control.

CLÉANTE. I wish there was a chance
   You two could somehow patch things up.

ELMIRE. If I'd realised the danger,
   I'd have been more reticent, and . . .

ORGON (to DORINE, seeing MONSIEUR LOYAL enter).
   Who's this? What does he want? Go and see.
   I'm in no fit state for visitors.

4. MONSIEUR LOYAL, MADAME PERNELLE,
   ORGON, DAMIS, MARIANE, DORINE, ELMIRE,
   CLÉANTE.

M. LOYAL. Dear sister, I must speak to Monsieur.

DORINE. He has company,
   And is not to be disturbed.

M. LOYAL. I shan't cause a nuisance.
  The reason for my visit won't displease him,
  Quite the reverse.

DORINE. Name please?

M. LOYAL. Just tell him, I've been sent for his own good
  By Monsieur Tartuffe.

DORINE (*to* ORGON).
  He seems alright. He's come from Tartuffe.
  It'll be to your advantage, he says.

CLÉANTE. Find out more. What exactly does he want?

ORGON. Perhaps he's offering a settlement.
  How should I act with him?

CLÉANTE. Stay tight-lipped,
  And if he talks peace, listen carefully.

M. LOYAL. Good day, Monsieur. May Heaven keep you from
  all harm,
  And bring you every blessing.

ORGON (*aside*). So far so good. This could well mean
  An agreement's in the air.

M. LOYAL. I've always admired this family;
  I was once in your father's employ.

ORGON. Forgive me, Monsieur, but have we met?
  I can't quite place you.

M. LOYAL. Loyal's the name, native of Normandy;
  Bailiff by trade, for my sins.
  For close on half a century now,

By the grace of God, I've done an honest job.
I'm here today, with your kind permission,
To serve you a writ . . .

ORGON. What!?

M. LOYAL. Let's not get excited;
It's just a summons, requiring you all
To remove yourselves and your belongings,
And make way forthwith for new occupants . . .

ORGON. Me, leave here?

M. LOYAL. Exactly. This house, as you're aware,
Belongs to good Monsieur Tartuffe –
As does everything you own.
This inventory will help;
You'll find it's as it should be.

DAMIS. How do you have the nerve . . . ?

M. LOYAL. This doesn't concern you.
I'm talking to Monsieur, who I'm sure
Believes in fair play. As a man of honour,
He'll want justice to be done.

ORGON. But . . .

M. LOYAL. I know, Monsieur, nothing in the world
Would make you contest
The order I'm entrusted with.
You're too much of a gentleman.

DAMIS. Those black robes don't impress me;
What you need's a damn good thrashing.

M. LOYAL.
> Your son should hold his tongue, Monsieur, or leave.
> There's such a thing as contempt of court.

DORINE. Monsieur Loyal, indeed! *Dis*loyal's his true name.

M. LOYAL. It's because I respect good men like you,
> Monsieur, that I took this case on.
> I can save you the unpleasantness
> Of having to deal with someone less friendly.

ORGON. What could be less friendly
> Than making people leave their house and home?

M. LOYAL. We're giving you time;
> You can have until tomorrow.
> All I require is to spend the night here,
> With ten of my men. We'll be no bother.
> Before we retire, please bring me
> The house-keys – a formality.
> I need nothing further;
> We can all sleep undisturbed.
> But, first thing tomorrow morning,
> Be ready to clear out everything.
> My men will help you; I specially chose
> Big, strapping lads for the task.
> I think I'm being very fair.
> I'd ask you to be the same, Monsieur;
> Let us get on with our job.

ORGON (*aside*). I'd give my last sou for the pleasure
> Of landing one great big punch on that ugly snout!

CLÉANTE. Careful.

DAMIS. Let me get at him,
   I can't hold back much longer!

DORINE. Fancy a taste of the lash, Monsieur Loyal?

M. LOYAL (*to* DORINE). You may live to regret that remark,
   My friend. The law applies to women too.

CLÉANTE. This is getting us nowhere.
   Monsieur, hand that piece of paper over,
   Then kindly leave.

M. LOYAL.
   Goodbye for now. The Lord preserve and keep you all.

ORGON. May you rot in Hell, you and the one who sent
   you!

5. ORGON, CLÉANTE, MARIANE, ELMIRE, MADAME
   PERNELLE, DORINE, DAMIS.

ORGON. So, mother, which of us was right? Go on,
   Read the writ; you'll find all the gory details.
   What do you think of him now?

MME. PERNELLE. I'm mortified. I don't know what to say.

DORINE. Aren't you being unfair? You mustn't blame him.
   He's doing it for God and for us poor sinners.
   Our salvation's his only concern.
   He knows that worldly things corrupt,
   So, out of pure charity, he's removed
   Every obstacle to your salvation.

ORGON. You don't know when to stop, do you?

CLÉANTE (*to* ORGON). We must make a plan of action.

ELMIRE. If we could expose his duplicity,
That would nullify the deed of gift.
Surely his treachery's so transparent
That it's no foregone conclusion he'll win?

6. VALÈRE, ORGON, CLÉANTE, ELMIRE, MARIANE,
MADAME PERNELLE, DAMIS, DORINE.

VALÈRE. Monsieur, I don't wish to add to your woes,
But things are going from bad to worse.
A good friend of mine,
Who knows of my attachment to your family,
Has broken his oath of official secrecy
To warn me you're in mortal danger.
You must flee at once, before it's too late.
That devil Tartuffe has double-crossed you;
He's just had an audience with the King,
And accused you of the gravest crime:
Shielding a known traitor to the State.
He's handed over that strong-box,
And now, you're wanted for treason by proxy.
An officer's en route as we speak,
Coming here to bring you in.
Tartuffe's showing him the way.

CLÉANTE. A classic case of *lèse majesté*.
Tartuffery triumphant; he's won.

ORGON. The man's not human.

VALÈRE. Please, don't delay; it would be fatal.
 My coach is waiting at the door,
 Plus a good supply of money.
 We mustn't wait; we must leave
 Before disaster strikes.
 I've found a safe house for you,
 And I'll take you there, if it'll help.

ORGON. I don't know how to thank you;
 Valère, I shan't forget this.
 God grant me the chance one day
 To repay you properly.
 (*To his family.*) Goodbye. Be careful to . . .

CLÉANTE. Just go; We'll take care of everything.

7. LAW OFFICER, TARTUFFE, VALÈRE, ORGON,
 ELMIRE, MARIANE, MADAME PERNELLE,
 DORINE, CLÉANTE, DAMIS.

TARTUFFE. Stop right there, Monsieur, where do you think
 you're going?
 We've got the perfect place for you nearby,
 At His Majesty's pleasure. You're under arrest.

ORGON. Traitor, you saved this one for last!
 The stab in the back, the perfect crime,
 The ultimate proof of a master!

TARTUFFE. Your insults can't disturb my peace of mind;
 Heaven has taught me to rise above pain.

CLÉANTE. Very stoical.

DAMIS. And convenient!

TARTUFFE. Don't waste your breath.
   I only heed the call of duty.

MARIANE. What a splendid job you've done;
   You'll be crowned in wreaths of glory!

TARTUFFE. The only glory I seek is to serve
   The wearer of the royal crown.

ORGON. Have you so quickly forgotten
   How I picked you up from the gutter?

TARTUFFE. I don't deny it;
   But my obligation to the King
   Is a duty I revere so much
   That all others go by the board.
   It calls for every sacrifice,
   Friends, parents, wife – even myself!

ELMIRE. The hypocrite!

DORINE. The slimy worm's got an answer for everything.

CLÉANTE. But if your sense of duty was so strong,
   Why did you wait till you'd been caught
   Trying to seduce Madame before you acted?
   Why not denounce Monsieur Orgon
   Before honour made him throw you out?
   I don't raise the matter of the gift
   To deter you from your duty –
   But if you'd already planned to accuse Orgon,
   Should you really have accepted it?

TARTUFFE (*to the* LAW OFFICER).
    Rid me of these bleating Jeremiahs;
    Let's get this business over with.

LAW OFFICER. Yes, we've been patient too long;
    I'm glad it's you that reminded me –
    My orders are to take you into custody.
    Come, your prison-cell awaits.

TARTUFFE. Who, me?

LAW OFFICER. Yes, you.

TARTUFFE. Why prison?

LAW OFFICER. You know exactly why.
    (*To* ORGON.) The panic's over, Monsieur. Rest assured,
    We live in an enlightened age. Our King,
    Who reads us like a book, hates any fraud;
    No plaster saint will ever take him in.
    His shrewd discernment is beyond compare;
    His searching gaze uncovers all deceit;
    To make sure that his judgement's really fair,
    He gathers in the facts till they're complete.
    While decent people prosper under him,
    His love of goodness doesn't cloud his sight.
    We've often heard him say no crime's as grim
    As foul hypocrisy, that deadly blight.
    If our impostor thought himself so smart,
    He hadn't reckoned with His Majesty.
    He saw his scheming from the very start –
    He's dealt with worse than this, believe you me!
    His expert eyes weren't fooled; they straightaway
    Saw the hideous face behind the mask.

To bring a suit against you was to play
Into our hands, and finish off the task.
Luck ran out for our master of disguise;
God ensured he made this crucial mistake.
No book's been printed of big enough size
To list the evil deeds of such a fake.
Disgusted by the rogue's ingratitude
And sheer contempt towards your family,
The King struck; his mounting disquietude
Wanted a solution, and speedily.
I came with Tartuffe to set him a trap;
If he felt quite safe, he'd relax his guard,
Make a false move – and then we'd have our chap!
We'd win the whole game on the final card.
Those papers Tartuffe claims are his by right,
I've been commanded to return to you;
Your deed of gift's annulled as from tonight,
By sov'reign decree, without more ado.
Finally, the King sees fit to ignore
The case of Argas, whom you befriended.
Your loyal valour in the recent war
Is not forgotten; the matter's ended.
Consider it a most deserved reward,
Virtue's honour, bestowed by virtue's Lord;
For merit's ever valued at its worth
By this, the wisest, fairest King on earth!

DORINE. Heaven be praised!

MME. PERNELLE. I can breathe again!

ELMIRE. What a happy *dénouement*!

MARIANE. Can you believe it?

ORGON (*to* TARTUFFE). Well, well, well! You monster . . .

CLÉANTE. No, brother, no!
  Where's your sense of dignity?
  Leave the poor sinner to his fate.
  He'll have enough remorse to cope with.
  Rehabilitation's the goal; he must come
  To hate his crimes, win back his self-respect.
  Then the King might shorten his sentence.
  Meanwhile, you should go on bended knee
  To thank our mighty monarch for his mercy.

ORGON. You're right; first things first. Let's throw ourselves
  At his feet, and praise his generosity.
  But afterwards, there's someone else
  Who merits *his* reward . . . I hereby give
  My daughter's hand to young Valère –
  No one so good, or so sincere!

The End.